Why This
Horse Won't
Drink

Why This Horse Won't Drink

How to Win— and Keep—Employee Commitment

A man may well bring a horse to the water,
But he cannot make him drinke without he will.
JOHN HEYWOOD
Proverbes

Ken Matejka

American Management Association

Library of Congress Cataloging-in-Publication Data

Matejka, Ken.
    Why this horse won't drink : how to win—and—keep employee
commitment / Ken Matejka.
        p. cm.
    Includes bibliographical references and index.
    ISBN 0-8144-5005-9 (hardcover)
    1. Employee motivation—United States.   2. Incentives in industry—
United States.   3. Personnel management—United States.   I. Title.
HF5549.5.M63M368   1990
    658.3'14—dc20   90-53215
                                                                                              CIP

Printing number

10   9   8

This book is dedicated to all the managers, students, and colleagues with whom I have had the pleasure of working over the years. Thanks for what you have learned and taught!

Contents

Acknowledgments

*T*here are many people I would like to thank for the successful completion of this book. First, many thanks to Sally and Anastasia for their patience, understanding, helpful suggestions, and indulgence when I needed to disappear onto the porch with my word processor to write down my thoughts. They never once complained.

To Dick Dunsing, who has written in tandem with me so often that it is hard to tell whose ideas are whose. Thanks for the help, encouragement, and permission to use some of our thoughts. To Neil Ashworth, Diane Dodd-McCue, Jay Liebowitz, Kurt Rethwisch, and John South, my other close colleagues and the coauthors of the articles quoted in this book. Thanks for your cooperation, ideas, and permission to use some of our material.

To Dean Glen Beeson and my chairperson, Bill Presutti, for giving me the release time that allowed me to write this book.

To Paul Meskanick, my graduate assistant, for his cheerfulness in undertaking some of the less than glamorous tasks I "dumped" on him.

To Carol Trozzo and Mary Lou Grasser, my trusty secretaries, who always seemed to make time for my work when I needed a quick turnaround.

To the editors of *Administrative Management, Clinical Laboratory Management Review, Journal of Managerial Psychology, Manage, Management Decisions, Management World, PACE, Personnel, Supervision,* and *Supervisory Management* for graciously giving me permission to use materials first published in their magazines. A complete list of the materials can be found at the back of this book.

To Adrienne Hickey, my editor at AMACOM, for having faith that "this horse would drink!"

Preface

For thousands of years, horse owners have looked for new and better ways of using and managing horses for profit and pleasure. With remarkable success, they have taught horses to jump over hedges, run through fire, and charge into the breach of a roaring cannon. Horses have been cajoled into pulling great weights, dancing to music (or at least appearing to), helping to bulldog cattle, and pulling sleighs across the snow. Horses have been carefully bred for different tasks: speed, appearance, jumping ability, strength, and endurance.

Horse owners have also had their failures. Horses have kicked their masters, thrown them, trampled them, gone north instead of south, or simply lain down in the middle of an adventurous quest. Whatever the sympathies between horse manipulator and horse, the ultimate defeat is aptly expressed in the proverb "You can lead a horse to water, but you can't make him drink!" Some horses won't go near the water. Some horses won't even pretend to drink. If they don't want to drink, they won't. Of course, we have no way of knowing what horses think in these moments of crisis, but it's amusingly clear what thoughts go through the minds of horse owners/riders:

"Why do I always get the bad horses?"
"Is that any way to treat your provider?"
"It's for his own good."
"Such an ungrateful horse."
"What a lazy horse."
"This horse is just trying to embarrass me."
"Why does my horse hate me? I love horses."
"This horse isn't well."
"You just can't buy a good horse these days."

And that's just the point! Owners often spend their time looking at behavior from their own viewpoint instead of from that of the horse. Most horses drink best when allowed to drink what they want, when they want, and how much they want. But some horses, left entirely to their own devices, don't drink at all, drink contaminated water, or drink too much—some even drink the right amount. In the ideal situation, someone who cares for the task and the horse will always provide good water and leave it to the horse—within limits!

Further, not all horses are the same. As the saying goes, "There are horses for courses." Some horses are docile and easy to tame and ride. Others are fiery and difficult. Some run better in the mud. Some prefer a fast track. Some horses respond best to rewards. Some need more discipline.

You may be wondering what all this has to do with managing people. We know that people are not horses. Their intellectual and psychological capabilities are far more complex. Their individual differences are also far greater.

The connection is that too many managers look at managing employees as if they were managing horses. They see employees' behavior from their own viewpoint and don't know (or care) what goes on in the minds of those they try to manage. If bad management practices don't work for horses, they certainly won't work for people. Frustration may cause managers to blame the "horse," but the truth is that many managers lack the knowledge needed to get this particular horse to drink. And, angry with themselves, they displace their anger onto the horse.

While motivation and performance must be approached from the employees' point of view because of individual differences, the rewards of caring stewardship, such as superior performance, accrue to the managers. Organizational life is about horses, people, managers, water, thirst, tasks, differences, and limits. It is also about metaphors (the horse and jockey), paradoxes (the selfish manager), and the unexpected (often an equitable solution). Remember, however, that it's a jungle out there. Survival and success go to managers who value their employees and therefore take the time to understand them while creatively turning them on to the task.

If horses could talk and get together to form unions when management failed them, horse training itself would have to change. Or would it? Isn't it alarming how many managers are rigid in their styles and ignorant about the nature, needs, and potential of their employees? That's why unions form. Employees don't vote *for* a union, they vote *against* management!

Some managers have simply become obsolete. The times have passed them by. Much of the old, autocratic style of management is useless in helping us to deal with a dynamic, competitive, global economy. For example, Likert's Linking Pin concept was an interesting idea about organization and coordination. But these days, as Tom Peters has pointed out in *Thriving on Chaos* (New York: Harper & Row, 1988), getting together to coordinate is often to "stall in the name of checking this out three layers up before acting." We can no longer afford these layers, luxuries, or games. We don't need linking pins, we need thinking pins! Regarding employees, we don't need animal trainers, we need quality gainers!

The horse is a beautiful, sensitive, caring, and intelligent animal and should be treated as such. But many managers aren't good horse trainers—much less good motivators of people. They fail to recognize differences and changes, and therefore never get past the problem of setting up consequences in a consistent, caring manner.

If you can't perform the basics well, you have little chance of moving on to the more complex issues of involvement, loyalty, and commitment—the issues that lead to superior levels of performance.

Why This
Horse Won't
Drink

1

The Path to
Human Performance

You can do anything you want in an organization—you just have to pay the consequences.

anaging the human variable in today's organizations can be frustrating or exhilarating, depending on your perspective. The typical employee is fairly easy to manage. In fact, most employees are quite capable of managing themselves. That may be the rub: Some managers are really superfluous at best and cause great harm at worst. Employees are much more capable than most managers ever realize. Employees simply act and react according to what they perceive as their own enlightened self-interest. Ergo, my first basic premise of managing human performance is an adaptation from the thoughts of B. F. Skinner:

Premise 1: Almost all employee behavior is purposeful and designed to bring employees the most pleasure and/or least pain, given (1) their perception of the options available to them, (2) their perception of the potential consequences for each action, and (3) their expectations regarding the behavior of others, especially that of their immediate supervisors.

From this premise, managing most employees is simply a matter of—

- identifying the behaviors that are critical to performance;
- mutually setting clear, reasonable goals;
- establishing and communicating potential rewards and disciplines;

- giving accurate, timely feedback;
- developing employee abilities to enhance performance;
- encouraging involvement through participation;
- inviting control through delegation;
- inspiring commitment through ownership and vision;
- administering rewards and disciplines as promised; and
- celebrating a job well done!

As the manager changes the potential rewards, behavior shifts. In many ways, it is that simple! For example, on the macro level, if you want to raise the savings rate in the United States, you merely provide incentives. Suppose that the first $10,000 of savings per family per year is tax-free. What do you think would happen? Bingo! Savings would increase. Then why isn't such a policy implemented? The answer provides the basis for premise 2.

Premise 2: The solutions to most organizational problems are readily apparent to almost everyone involved, but nothing much is done because a continuation of the problem is actually preferable to the alternatives.

For example, suppose a manager is having trouble managing her time. Fire fighting is prevalent. Do we send her to a time management seminar? Curiously enough, time management usually isn't the issue. Most managers already know much more about time management than they practice. Typically, the real issue is change. Until the pain of continuing to fight fires gets too great, or the rewards for changing become enticing enough, things will stay as they are.

Between sessions at a management development seminar that we were leading last summer, a colleague and I were discussing the apparent desire of a particular state to change its image by enticing more artists to move there. No problem! It would be done tomorrow by providing subsidized housing for artists and by exempting them from state income taxes. It will, of course, probably never happen. The state politicians know the answer, but they aren't that serious about making it happen. Pretending to want change is the real issue.

Why do organizations that know that incentive compensation plans work fairly well as a means of encouraging performance have systems that pay for position? Entitlement pay plans prevail in the Fortune 500, it was learned from a study I conducted in 1989.[1]

The bottom line is that most organizations are concerned more with the status quo, managerial style, cultural norms, and "satisficing" than with "maximizing." When a decent compensation system is set up and workers begin to buy into it and perform well, thereby making more money, it won't be long before someone in a white shirt and tie talks the company into changing the standards. The workers are making too much money, so the standards must be wrong. And herein lies the beginning of the end of trust between labor and management. Besides, the alternative is to have to think hard about how to creatively implement the incentive system with other types of workers. That's tough stuff. Why not just destroy the new system, get performance back to average levels, and be happier?

Premise 3: Ownership and vision build commitment. The entire American free enterprise system is built on the idea of private property (ownership of the tools of production) and the freedom to pass it on through inheritance. As functioning members of this society, almost all of us treasure ownership. When I own it, I take care of it; the business is a reflection of me. For an explanation of the shoddy nature of some American goods and services these days, look no farther than to the caretakers at the top (not entrepreneurs) and a disenfranchised work force. Because they are told that they just work there and are treated accordingly, it is not surprising that employees develop an "it's not my job, Man" mentality.

What Lies Ahead: A True Double-Entendre

People in American organizations are working hard, but not necessarily at the right things. Part One of this book explores some of the things our executives, managers, and employees are diligently pursuing instead of managing optimum performance. These misdirected but reinforced endeavors are affectionately called "diseases of excellence." These organizational "scams" are funny when you see them for what they are.

Part Two explains how to increase the "effort" of employees by understanding and properly administering rewards and discipline. Chapters 5–9 unravel the perceptual issues and resulting frustrations and deal with how to choose appropriate and fair rewards, when to apply consequences, how to keep communication barriers at a minimum, and, finally, how to set up programs that will build trust and change behavior.

Part Three addresses those unusual people who seem to fall between the cracks. Problem people don't fit the typical behavioral patterns. Whether it's you, a baffling boss, a difficult employee, or getting things done in groups, Chapters 10–13 should help you to turn on turned-off people.

Finally, effort alone won't necessarily translate into high performance. Part Four explains how to take the effort generated in Part Two and combine it with increased involvement and empowerment to gain commitment and increase organizational performance. After all is said and done, it's time to celebrate the successes!

Are There Any Questions?

Sometimes we are our own worst enemies. While I think I can show that I know a great deal about what should be done, I make mistakes just like everyone else. My hope is merely to make fewer mistakes than most people.

For example, I guess it's just the models provided by my professors and my own conditioning, but for fifteen years I ended my university classes by asking if there were any questions. How mindless that was! Who was motivated by this exercise? Me! Most of the students were motivated to leave for their next class. If a student asked a question, he was often perceived as a villain by his classmates. The social pressure in the room was to be quiet so we could leave on time (or a little early) and get to our next class or work situation. The inquisitive student kept the class late and was punished by his peers in the hall afterwards. Rather than admonishing the class for not being willing to participate, I finally saw the ludicrousness of my request. Now, I simply announce that as soon as I get three good questions we will leave. The inquisitive student now becomes a hero or heroine for (1) facilitating the class's learning while (2) facilitating its leaving. Life is so simple if you think about it!

The path to human performance has five steps:

1. The *Contradictions*. Assess what you are doing instead of what you know you should be doing.
2. The *Consequences*. Motivate through clear targets, rewards, and disciplines.
3. The *Contacts*. Communicate consequences effectively.
4. The *Contraries*. Assess and manage the problem people, including yourselves.
5. The *Commitments*. Manage employee participation, development, involvement, and ownership.

This book is about—

- how easy this process is; and
- what keeps it from being easy!

Note

1. Ken Matejka and Elaine McGivern, "A Fortune 500 Survey of Current Managerial Compensation Plans," *1989 Proceedings of the International Academy of Management and Marketing*, pp. 21–26.

Action Exercise

Take a few moments and think about each element below. How much do you think you know about each factor? Your thoughts will, of course, be subjective. Some managers will do better than others. But what is most important is to be honest in your responses. What variables do you need to understand better?

Factors	Perfect Knowledge									No Knowledge
You	10	9	8	7	6	5	4	3	2	1	0
Employees	10	9	8	7	6	5	4	3	2	1	0
Tasks	10	9	8	7	6	5	4	3	2	1	0
Organization	10	9	8	7	6	5	4	3	2	1	0

Degree of Skill	The Best									The Worst
Communicating	10	9	8	7	6	5	4	3	2	1	0
Establishing rapport	10	9	8	7	6	5	4	3	2	1	0
Motivating others	10	9	8	7	6	5	4	3	2	1	0
Dealing with problem people	10	9	8	7	6	5	4	3	2	1	0
Delegating	10	9	8	7	6	5	4	3	2	1	0
Developing commitment	10	9	8	7	6	5	4	3	2	1	0

Now comes the tough question: How would your subordinates rate you on these factors? The litmus test is the congruency between your perceptions and those of your employees. Why not give your subordinates a blank copy of the exercise and test the level of agreement as to your skills?

If your subordinates' rating of you adds up to 90–100, you don't need this book. Pass it on to someone who does! But if your subordinates' rating of you is such that your total is less than 90, I believe this book can help you to understand why.

One

What Are We Doing Instead of Managing Performance?

Priorities are in the "I" of the beholder.

When a horse is led to water and doesn't drink, there are many possible explanations. The behavior (refusing to drink) is not the problem but a symptom. The cause may be internal or external. Internal reasons can vary from lack of thirst to obstinance to fear. External causes can vary from improper rewards and punishments to conflicting goals or barriers to the goal.

Most managers actually treat horses more fairly and consistently than they treat employees. What would you think if you were a horse and I told you to head toward the water and then held a bunch of carrots in the opposite direction? Confusing, isn't it? We wouldn't do that to a horse, would we? Then why do we do it to people?

Some managers tell employees that they want cooperation, then turn around and reward selfish behavior. As if this weren't bad enough, they follow up by yelling at them for not cooperating. Confusing? You bet! Perhaps even worse is when management tells employees to take care of customers and then proceeds to write and distribute a bunch of policies, rules, and procedures that prevent, or at least seriously delay, anyone from servicing the customers) This is analogous to the rider sneaking out in the middle of the night to build a huge wall around the water and then taking the horse out the next morning, leading him to the wall, ordering him to drink, and finally (the coup de grace), punishing him for not drinking when told. I suggest to you that this example is ludicrous, inane—and real!

Horses aren't always rational, but then neither are human beings. Horses have likes, dislikes, preferences, and priorities. So do people. Besides the incompatible behaviors mentioned, managers and employees alike often use a distorted decision-making process. They have biases, and favorites. But unlike horses, humans have value systems that affect their decisions.

Based on their values and priorities, humans often pick their favorite person or option very early in the process but then pretend to keep searching. Next, they distort new alternatives and construct a set of criteria that make the favorite decision look superior. This decision-making model was dubbed the "implicit favorite," and documented in a well-known study of job selection by students graduating from M.I.T.'s Sloan School of Management.[1] The author discovered that most students quickly identified the job that was most desirable to them but pretended to search even after receiving an offer from their preferred company. It became apparent that additional jobs were being used to justify their favorite as the best possible selection. Soelberg found that 87 percent of the students studied eventually chose their initial favorites.

Many of the managers I have worked with seem to follow this "rationalizing," rather than "rational," decision-making process. There are three important components of this behavior. First, an early emotional choice, based on the manager's values and priorities, is made. Second, the manager tries to convince everyone (including herself) that she is continuing to search for an option according to an objective set of criteria. Third, the manager gathers the facts and statistics and comparisons that help support her initial choice.

Most important management decisions occur under conditions of uncertainty in which not all the information, alternatives, and probabilities are known. The result is that most managerial issues are decided quickly based on subjective criteria while great effort is expended on giving the appearance of "seeking truth." I can attest to the fact that subjectivity is alive and well, even in our universities!

    At this point, I am not evaluating the choice of subjective over objective criteria; I am merely pointing out that it is prevalent. This process helps explain my second premise from Chapter 1, that though the solutions to most organizational problems are apparent to almost everyone, nothing is done to implement them. The game is to pretend to do something, when, in fact, the desire is for things to remain the same.

Let me illustrate by giving two examples of how this "scam" works with respect to productivity and creativity.

What's All the Fuss About Productivity?

It's difficult to pick up a recent business publication without encountering articles on productivity and/or creativity. Productivity is important, and deceptively seductive, but it is not the true crux of the problem facing business. The United States is the most productive industrial nation in the history of the world. Although productivity is vital and warrants continual attention and improvement, the paramount competitive issue is creating value for the price. Productivity is important insofar as it relates to keeping the costs and price low, but the perception of value at that price is what determines purchases. Quality is the more prevalent concern, and people usually determine quality. The concern for productivity over quality by the automakers is precisely what has caused the precipitous decline of the American auto industry. The automakers did exactly what they set out to do—push as many cars off the end of the assembly line as they could. They were immensely successful.

If you want to know what the real priorities are, just ask a production worker to number the following goals in order of their importance to management: quantity, cost, quality, and safety. The workers on the firing line know what counts. They have learned the hard way.

How Creative Are We?

The second issue, creativity, is closely related to quality. To be competitive in the current global climate, an organization must be creative and flexible, as several authors have eloquently pointed out again and again. Judging from the number of articles on creativity, it is obvious that editors and writers think it is a great idea whose time has come. But what are American companies doing about it? In the Fortune 500 survey mentioned in Chapter 1, the emphasis on creativity was appallingly absent. Less than 40 percent of the companies claimed even to be innovative in their philosophical leanings. Three out of four companies said they had no innovative monetary compensation plans, and two-thirds of them did not even offer any nonmonetary managerial compensation plans like management participation, involvement teams, or quality circles for management. Over half these companies had no formal rewards for creativity or innovation, and 70 percent lacked even a formal suggestion system. Clearly, while creativity is being voiced, it is not yet being reinforced in any sweeping manner by our largest companies. There are some organizations that have been and continue to be creative, but they are in the minority, even amidst the recent barrage of opinions on the need for creativity and innovation.

How Are We Shooting Ourselves in the Foot?

Whereas management writers as diverse as McGregor, Herzberg, Locke, Lawler, and Peters agree that rewards must be linked to the desired behavior, compensation continues to be used to support past performance and position rather than as an incentive to future action. This is not surprising! Just as U.S. automakers rejected the ideas of Dr. W. Edwards Deming, American industries have a history of accepting what they want to believe rather than what is true. Meanwhile, corporate experiments such as the GM NUMMI plant, the Nissan plant in Smyrna, Tennessee, and the Skippy Peanut Butter plant in Little Rock, Arkansas, are thriving examples of what could be. Cooperation, trust, and decision making are pushed all the way down the line, quality is emphasized, and reinforcement of creative, continual improvements abound. Experiments in which workers gain some control over their tasks are apparently very threatening to management. Perhaps that explains why some truly innovative projects remain "secrets" that management considers best left untold.

The truth seems to be that as the answers come into clearer focus, many of our executives, managers, and employees are dearly holding on to their old "favorite" methods. Each group works hard, but expends energy on behaviors that are often counterproductive to superior corporate performance. These behaviors continue because they are reinforced. Each group perpetuates its own "diseases of excellence," which are fervently pursued instead of gains in quality, creativity, and performance.

Chapters 2 through 4 describe the ailments that are keeping us from being the best we can be. These "diseases" are what our executives, managers, and employees concentrate on instead of managing the truly important aspects of performance. They represent the contradictions between what we know we should be doing and our actual behavior.

Note

1. P. O. Soelberg, "Unprogrammed Decision Making," *Industrial Management Review*, Vol. 8 (1967), pp. 19–29.

Corporate Diseases
of Excellence

Luck must exist. How else can we explain the success of our competitors?

As a consumer, I can attest to the fact that the United States has some great companies. No one provides service better than Disney, IBM, or Domino's Pizza. No one stresses innovation more than 3M or Neiman-Marcus. No one provides better value for the price than L. L. Bean, Wal-Mart, or Wendy's. And no one understands managing human resources better than Hewlett-Packard. However, in today's chaotic business setting, not even these leaders are safe. No company has the luxury of a safe lead. Additionally, the "champion to has-been" cycle is becoming shorter. If complacent, today's excellent firm becomes tomorrow's dinosaur. The once-dominant U.S. Olympic basketball team winning the bronze medal is similar to what has happened in the business community. The rest of the world is catching up quickly. Sadly, today's excellent U.S. companies are in the minority. Most are too encumbered with what I call "diseases of excellence" to excel.

Webster defines *disease* as "a condition that impairs the health." Corporate diseases are ailments that damage organizational health. These corporate ailments can cost the country dearly in terms of lost jobs, lost profits, lost markets, and lost exports. Corporate diseases of excellence occur when great amounts of effort are expended on being excellent at unimportant things, or excellent in the wrong directions. Athletes know that when they overdo some types of training, they risk a physical breakdown. Corporate diseases of excellence represent break-downs that occur because the company overtrains on certain activities. Many corporations are trying desperately to perpetuate many activities and behaviors that they dearly love but that are counterproductive when overemphasized. Some of these pet systems won't work unless there are expanding, captive markets. Of course, in expanding, captive markets, almost anything works. It is curious that most of our organizational and management models come from the military, which is in a monopolistic position and provides a service unlike that provided by any other organization. Getting a battalion across the Alps in winter and in record time with thousands of lives at stake and perhaps the future of the free world riding on the event is not the same as making quality hamburgers.

Interestingly enough, corporate diseases of excellence are readily apparent to bystanders, but are not generally open to public discussion or subject to change. Questioning the powers that be about these sacred cows will usually result in—

- a knowing smile (implying now naïve you are);
- followed by a tried and true, red-white-and-blue slogan— "That's just the way it is in the real world!" or "We've always done it that way!";
- followed by the implication that you have a bright future in this company unless you continue to question these sacred cows.

You see, corporate diseases of excellence are now part of the very fabric of many American companies and to question them is to question America, by golly.

The following "magnificent seven" corporate diseases of excellence are representative of the major illnesses that are preventing many U.S. corporations from being better. The common thread running through these afflictions is a great expenditure of time and energy on misplaced priorities, which leads to a loss of employee commitment, which leads to a loss of quality, which leads to a loss of customers and markets.

Disease 1: Corporate Elephantiasis

Early in our childhood, insecurity precipitates the beginning of the "mine is bigger than yours!" game. The game starts with toys, teddy bears, daddies, and cookies. Later in life it shifts to cars, spouses, offices, and houses. The United States, as a young, insecure nation in a large land full of bountiful natural resources, found it easy to slip into this mentality. As the new kid on the block without the history and experience that Europe had, it was attractive to claim that ours was bigger than anyone else's. So the country grew and the companies grew. Bigger is better, as Texas (and later Alaska) would claim.

Webster defines *paradox* as "a seemingly contradictory, un-believable, or absurd statement that may actually be true." The paradox here is that in our current chaotic world, small may be better quality, less costly, and more profitable. In a study that reviewed hundreds of other studies, economists Walter Adams and James Brock proposed that bigness has not delivered on its promises and concluded that "scientific evidence has not been kind to the apostles of bigness and to their mythology."[1] As one example, Adams and Block quote a study by Frederic Scherer involving fifteen former subsidiaries of conglomerates that had been sold to their former managers; of these, fourteen exhibited substantial profit improvements despite the debt incurred in the buyouts.

As the firm grows and diversifies, the fear of losing control brings more controls. The irony is that more controls internally often result in less control in the marketplace. Big usually brings permanence, predictability, and policies. Small often brings agility, mobility, and flexibility.

Disease 2:   Corporate Short-Term-Itis

Boards of directors and corporate executives have also contributed greatly to perhaps the single most widespread disease in corporate America—"short-term-itis." The United States is a melting pot of diverse peoples, cultures, and values. Because of these differences, perhaps, the nation as a whole has never gone in for long-term planning. The only time we seem to pull together is when we are threatened from outside. Perhaps the best example of planning in the United States is its space program. Here we have a long-term, cooperative effort between government and business. But it was precipitated and perpetuated by the Cold War and the Soviet Union's launching of Sputnik. Suddenly, we perceived a threat and responded. Lately, in our freeze-dried, microwave world, in which we can watch World War III on TV being started, fought, and won in three hours with forty-one commercial breaks, instant gratification is expected. It should be easy to turn anything around in the morning.

Companies perpetuate short-term-itis through their lack of planning and the short-run nature of their compensation systems. Compensation is the single most important link between expectations and behavior. CEOs are hired and charged with trying to improve the company's quarterly profits and dividends. If they succeed, they can be heroes and collect their bonuses. This short-run outlook and incentive system stemming from the very top of the organization can cause a CEO to mortgage the future of the company. Games such as "return on assets" are won by depleting the asset base and moving on to another company before the roof caves in. Games such as "improving the quarterly profits" may result in cutting down on the very expenses that could save the company in the long run, such as R&D, employee development, or marketing. Resource deployment becomes a different issue when success in the short term is the goal.

In the Fortune 500 companies I studied, the emphasis was on rewarding for position and past performance, not on incentives for future behavior. Almost three-fourths of the companies perceived their compensation plans as paying for position rather than as paying for results. Furthermore, most of the companies admitted that their appraisal instruments were mainly based on short-run, subjective criteria. Short-term-itis is alive and well!

When evaluation is based on short-term numerical accomplishments, innovation and sustainable competitive advantage usually die. The trick to contracting this disease is: (1) pretending that the corporation's constituencies must be treated in the prioritized order of stockholders, customers, and employees in the short run; and (2) convincing everyone that stockholders only invest for the short run and that they prefer dividends to long-run stock appreciation. The strategies for perpetuating this disease take many forms. Pay dividends instead of reinvesting; acquire a company rather than build one; market producible products rather than produce marketable products; specialize for productivity rather than for quality; and evaluate the top staff on short-run numbers. These strategies will almost ensure short-run, risk-free suboptimization.

Disease 3: Corporate Amnesia

Most large, publicly held corporations don't know who they are anymore. As private companies grow, the leader is the founder, the driving force, and owner. They grow because they know the business and provide more value per dollar than their competitors. But as they turn public and the founders are replaced by "caretakers," the direction of the corporation begins to change. Where once the mission was simple and clear, and the company was close to its customers by necessity, the new lumbering giant, led by a professional manager, begins to lose sight of who it is and how it got there. As these companies grow and experience professional management changes, they develop corporate amnesia, a loss of continuity resulting in a gap in the corporate memory. A sense of "the business" is replaced by a "financial mentality," which turns the company into a diversified organization that looks like fifty other similar companies. The history and, more important, the competitive edge are often lost. Rather than creating new product uses and value, the manager treats the business simply as a "cash cow" and milks it while looking at new investment opportunities; eventually he winds up selling the business. Have you noticed how Americans have given up on and gotten out of so many industries? Take automobiles. The country that put a man on the moon can't make a decent small car. It was widely reported that after GM purchased EDS, and Ross Perot, as a new GM board member, suggested that a company with GM's financial resources should be able to make a competitive small car quickly, he was swiftly labeled an outsider who didn't understand the nature of automobile manufacturing.

As top management changes, so do the values that are the driving force behind corporate priorities and goals. Most middle managers, when asked to write down the mission, values, and goals of their corporation, have great difficulty naming them. How can employees all move in the same direction when their managers cannot even clearly state that direction? Clarity is job 1! Commitment is job 2! Quality is job 3! Our corporations have lost their identity, and their clarity. Corporate amnesia has contributed greatly to the loss of competitive advantage.

Disease 4:   Corporate Dyslexia

Is employee happiness important? Some managers couldn't care less about the morale of their workers. They are ignorant of the benefits of sharing and caring. Other managers have the mistaken notion that it is the manager's job to make subordinates happy. These managers are ignorant of the facts. The relationship between happiness and performance is a tricky one that must be clearly understood. The employee decides from his own perceptions how much job satisfaction exists and whether this company and this boss are pleasant to encounter. Performance is a comparison between actual behavior and the manager's expectations. The perception of satisfaction is in the "I" of the employee. The perception of performance is in the "I" of the manager.

Which comes first, happiness or performance? That is, are happy workers more productive or are productive workers happier? Many managers would argue that happy workers perform better. But this contradicts need theories, which claim that unfilled needs are motivators. The studies conducted would suggest that while there is no clear correlation between the level of happiness and future performance levels, the proper sequence is probably that high performance (as perceived by the manager) accompanied by equitable rewards (as perceived by the employee) will result in satisfaction.[2] Clear goals, adequately rewarded when accomplished, will raise the level of effort next time. Trust increases the next performance. The keys to the process are to relate to all workers in a fair, consistent way, to challenge them, and to reward their performance with things that are meaningful to them.

Disease 5:   Corporate Rigor Mortis

Hierarchical systems with many layers don't work well in dynamic, competitive situations. Hierarchies have built-in inflexibilities. Holding up the great and growing American pyramid is giving many managers a hierarchical hernia. Specialization has developed "empire building" into a new American art form.

A great example of the effects of specialization is the distance it places between people in the same company. Have you ever called a company and tried to speak to the person you most need to talk to but received the big runaround? Nobody knows whom you should talk to because they don't encounter each other and may even be charged with pursuing different, often conflicting goals. Corporate rigor mortis has taken hold!

The real "function" of the overabundance of clerks, accountants, lawyers, planners, and other staff managers is to increase the cost of the product or service. Each area forms an interest group to protect and proliferate its own kind. If someone can't get promoted, building an empire beneath himself will at least increase his compensation entitlements. To these people, goals mean personal goals. Nothing kills vitality and responsiveness like layers of people. Boxing in employees with elaborate job descriptions helps build the empire mentality and prevents employees from being able to respond. Remember, carpenters can't do masonry, masons can't fool with electric wires, electricians dare not touch plumbing, and so on. While these separations have reasons for being, the result is that instead of one person being able to finish the job, four craftsmen have to be transported to the scene to finish the work. That's pretty expensive logic. On top of this, how much do you think a salary expert, cost accountant, corporate lawyer, or billing clerk knows about the production department and its problems? How can they all possibly be pulling in the same direction?

It's ironic that corporations of late have begun to cut out some of the management fat and to cross-train a few people. Not because they listened to the experts and saw it coming, but because they have been hammered so badly by the competition that they are forced to cut costs. Even here they sometimes screw up by dismissing the highest-paid people to cut costs the most. This sends a clear message to the troops: If you work hard and play the game the way it was designed, you will be rewarded by dismissal. Now doesn't that make you want to run right out and work your head off for this organization? Cutting costs because excessive expenses shouldn't be tolerated makes sense. Cutting costs to try to compete with a factory in Taiwan is ludicrous.

Disease 6:   Corporate Cannibalism

Competition is part of the beauty of a capitalistic system. Competition between companies brings vitality and innovation, and benefits the consumer through better quality and/or lower prices. But competition within the company is very overrated. The paradox is that increasing external competition requires increasing internal cooperation. The Japanese have it right. Provide the best product possible. Satisfy the customer by creating more value. Compete with your competitors. Direct the competition outward. Cooperate within the company.

In a typical American company, there is more competition encouraged within the company than is directed at competitors. The system is individualistic. It is a virtue that man, the animal, does not eat his/her young. This civility often does not hold in the corporate setting. A survival-of-the-fittest mystique permits you to make fair game of anyone who gets in your way. This cannibalism is not literal, but figurative. Managers don't kill their subordinates; managers dehumanize them, stifle their careers, steal their ideas. What organizations often condone is cannibalizing careers, not people.

This internal competition is costing us dearly. Companies pit employee against employee, department against department, and boss against subordinate. The reward structure encourages individual characteristics and achievements. These organizations operate internally with a win-lose rather than a win-win mentality. In an individualistic company, the "rising star" is the person who, in the short run, has achieved the most personal glory. In a group-oriented firm, the "rising star" is the one who has made the decisions that best advance overall company objectives.

Disease 7:   Corporate Cultural Blindness

The attitude that you, your company, your culture, and/or your country is at the center of the universe is potentially very debilitating. There is nothing wrong with patriotism, loyalty, or self-confidence. But when these factors prevent you from being able to learn from others, you have tied one hand behind your back unnecessarily. This mental set is even more dangerous when the feeling that "what worked here will work anywhere" is adopted.

Why bother studying different cultures, history, languages, or organizations? Corporate cultural blindness is convenient. Let them study us! If I have an idea that is an 8 on a scale of 1 to 10, and you study my idea and improve upon it, making it a 9, what do we have? I have an 8 and you have a 9. Guess who wins?

The Japanese successes have surprised and confused us. Sometimes we view them with admiration, sometimes with fear. Basically, we don't understand them. The Japanese study English, but we don't study Japanese. The Japanese have been sending students to American universities for decades to study our gurus and culture. Only recently have we begun to see the importance of learning about them.

Cultural blindness might be more subtly applied when business ventures outside the United States are viewed as secondary to domestic efforts, even when profit margins warrant the reverse. We tend to fear what we do not understand. And there is a great deal in the world that we have never taken the time to understand.

A spin-off of cultural blindness is an attitude of helplessness and hopelessness. Here the holy grail is host-country-oriented. The manager is so overwhelmed by the differences between the operating environments that he gives up and believes that the other country has all the advantages. So why try? Just do what they do.

Neither of these attitudes is appropriate for maximizing your organization's position.

A Capsule for Diseases

Diseases of excellence are caused by great expenditures of energy in the wrong directions. Our executives are not lazy, just misguided. We are now suffering from the misdirections and the fatigue brought about by our exertions. We have built up big biceps to run a marathon.

We need to view our organizations differently and put the systems in place that will encourage the behavior needed, not substantiate our pet peeves. We need to take care of the people who take care of the customers and products. Employees treat customers the way they get treated.

Specialization is a tool. Used to excess, it polarizes workers, alienates customers, lowers quality, and removes identity. Forced to acknowledge these facts, our automobile manufacturers are beginning to break down some of the walls created by job specialization and to construct a workplace where knowledge, not specialization, is demanded.

Of course, if you mention any of these corporate diseases in your company, you may encounter that knowing smile and "nothing can be done about these things" response. That's what people with a vested interest in these ailments say!

Notes

1. Walter Adams and James Brock, *The Bigness Complex: Industry, Labor and Government in the American Economy* (New York: Pantheon Books, 1986), pp. 44–46.
2. For example, see E. E. Lawler III, "Developing a Motivating Work Climate," *Management Review*, Vol. 66 (1977), p. 26.

Action Exercise

How prevalent are these "corporate diseases of excellence" in your organization? Use the chart below to rank the order of prevalence of these ailments in your own setting.

Rank Order	Disease	Area of Your Organization in Which This Malady Is Most Prevalent
_____	Elephantiasis	_____
_____	Corporate amnesia	_____
_____	Short-term-itis	_____
_____	Corporate dyslexia	_____
_____	Rigor mortis (Hierarchical hernias)	_____
_____	Corporate cannibalism	_____
_____	Cultural blindness	_____

If you work in a large organization (where you won't be easily identified) and you have a sense of humor, why not initiate a Corporate Disease of the Month Award and post it on the bulletin board as a means of raising awareness of inconsistencies and misdirections?

If you find peers, superiors (interesting word, huh?), or subordinates who understand and agree with needed changes, don't forget to reinforce this insight whenever you have the opportunity.

Managerial Diseases
of Excellence

Every management trainee ought to be required to take Mind Reading 101 before reporting to work to be prepared for the real world!

*H*aving poked some fun at the corporation and its top executives in the preceding chapter, I may as well move on to the other managers. (You didn't think they would go unscathed, did you?) Another factor contributing to suboptimal human performance in American companies is managerial diseases of excellence. How can so many managers be expending so much energy with so little result? Why are so many employees turned off?

As you glance at your Seiko watch, get in your Nissan Z, and listen to your Hitachi speakers, on the way home to watch your Sony TV, by the comfort of your Sanyo air conditioning, do you ever think about what it all means? While it is difficult to generalize, the Japanese seem to manage workers better than we do. (Perhaps it's because they haven't had as much practice at it as we have.) The rosy picture of the Japanese company is, of course, exaggerated. But even in the United States, with American workers, it appears that some Japanese companies achieve more commitment, more loyalty, higher morale, and higher quality than most U.S. companies do.

Why? Time and effort aren't the answers. Our managers work just as long and just as hard. We are failing not for lack of effort but for lack of understanding. Most of the time, our managers don't appear to value employees very much. Of course, after helping organized labor come into existence through mismanagement, and then having to deal with the "union mentality" for so many years, their perspective may be quite understandable.

Most managers don't really understand people. They are too busy with "more important" technical tasks to study people. The only time some managers think about the employees is when they need something done. Our work force is crying out for meaningful work, but doesn't have it. Our reward systems are so out of sync with what is needed that "problem employees" abound. How can you have an appropriate and effective appraisal and reward system and still have problem employees? Wouldn't the system have caught and dealt with them?

Many American managers expend great energy in the wrong pursuits. Like corporate diseases, managerial diseases hinder human performance in organizations. These malaises are just as costly, as readily apparent, and as seldom addressed as corporate diseases are.

In the rest of this chapter, I present the "sensational six," or what I believe are the six most common and harmful managerial diseases of excellence as they relate to turning off employees.

Disease 1:   Management by Mind Reading

One of my all-time favorites, and one I have inadvertently used on many occasions, is management by mind reading. This disease is simple enough. Just have something in mind that you keep as your own little secret until you spring it on an unsuspecting employee. Make my day! Guess what I'm thinking! Requiring mind reading of your employees is great fun, quick, calls for little energy, and can really stroke your ego. It is the industrial equivalent of a professor offering the following final exam question: "What was I thinking of when I wrote this question?" Folly? Frustrating? The manager holds the power of information leading to the rewards or sanctions. Management by telepathy is so ingrained because it is self-reinforcing. It rewards ESP rather than performance and insidiously invalidates performance appraisals.

Consider the following three examples of mind reading modes.

Manager A:	"Every employee of mine should know what's expected of him. I shouldn't have to

spend my time spelling it out." Wouldn't it be terrible if you told your subordinates exactly what you wanted? Good grief, they might just go ahead and do it. That would create a real dilemma because then they would expect to be rewarded. Worse yet, maybe all your employees would perform well. What would you then do about appraising them, especially when top management uses a forced distribution system in which 20 percent of your subordinates *must* be rated as poor?

Manager B: "I shouldn't have to spend my time walking around praising people. They should know when I'm pleased." This variation on mushroom management ("Keep them in the dark") guarantees that employees will be confused, frustrated, and praise-deprived!

Manager C: "Why doesn't Mary understand how I feel? Although I haven't told her yet, if she says that to one more customer, she is in deep trouble!" Mary is, of course, unaware of her manager's expectations. Her behavior will not change, especially since she has been doing things this way for some time with no negative feedback.

The Antidote: Be straight with your people. Privately held expectations are a curse for the manager and set subordinates up for ultimate failure and the accompanying negative feedback. Expecting some behavior without asking for it is as illogical as it is traditional. Management by mind reading frustrates even your most conscientious people.

Give your people a clear definition of their jobs, their work relationships, and the results you expect from them. Employees respect managers who are honest and consistent. So:

- Talk straight.
- Expect only what you clearly and directly ask for.
- Focus on performance, not pet peeves.

- To get more, try adding "why" to your "what."
- Give frequent feedback.
- Praise what goes well.

The bottom line is that if managers don't have enough respect for their subordinates to communicate directly and clearly with them, they don't deserve to receive much help in meeting their goals. Unfortunately, to many managers, these games of peeka-boo and hide-and-seek are more important to their own esteem than increased performance is.

Disease 2: The Malady of Macho Management

One very popular management disease is macho management. You don't have to be a man to be a macho manager (although it sure helps). You just have to be a hard-driving, take no prisoners, work your butt off, shoot from the hip, ride herd on the little people, full speed ahead, ready-fire-aim manipulator. This type of manager thrives because many corporate cultures nurture the macho behavior. These managers have great impact because it takes only a few machos, carefully placed, to prevent the company from dealing with reality. Finally, macho managers are costly because their energy is displaced from progress to building the macho myth.

Macho managers are much more concerned with maintaining their reputation for strength and endurance than with building a high-talent team that achieves through collaboration and focused efforts. Damaging the career of a competing peer is sometimes a higher priority than taking creative steps to ensure the success of the company. Macho managers utilize three specific gimmicks to build their facade: (1) style, (2) strategies, and (3) slogans.

The Macho Manager's Style

Macho managers are experts at selling the sizzle. Perception and appearance are much more important to them than substance. Create the illusion! The macho manager's style consists of power, paranoia, protection, protégés, and performance.

Power, or the perception of power, is central to the macho manager's image. Look as if you're in control! In control of yourself, the job, and the organization. Speak when you could listen. Scold when you could nurture. Walk when you could ride. Run when you could walk. Stand when you could sit. Work when you could relax. Activity equals results! Don't let people finish speaking; cut them off in anticipation of what they will say and have your rebuttal ready. Show no mercy. Take no prisoners. Sympathy is for wimps.

Paranoia is a necessary component of the macho style. Whether it's the unions, the competition, or the department next door, always be on guard because "they're out to get you!" Life is a constant vigil. Never let your guard down. Macho managers are always alert, their hands on their guns, their backs to the wall, positioned so that the sun is in their opponents' eyes. Whether it's the next car on the freeway or the next manager down the hall, get them first.

Protection is a spin-off of paranoia. If they're out to get you, you can never be open, honest, or receptive. Wimps are open and honest. Macho managers never share their feelings for fear that the truth will be used as a weapon against them. Deception is critical. Never let anyone know that you are doing anything but "great!"

Protégés are powerful heirs. Whether it be Vince Lombardi, General Patton, or John Wayne, choose a role model who is supermasculine. Western film stars, war heroes, and tough sports personalities work best. Acquire a picture of one of them and place it over your desk to tell the world you're tough as nails. Use their language: "Conduct a strategic campaign," "Carve up their defense," "Penetrate their line." Within the company, create the perception that you are tight with the most powerful people.

Performance is the final piece in the puzzle of a macho manager. Time is valuable. It must be used, spent, and manipulated. Every act is a performance and every event is a potential act. If you run out of performance goals at work, hurry home to attack a household project or lead the Pony League team to the title. Never rest—someone might be gaining on you! Hit the target hard and move on to the next goal. Above all, never take a break, never let up! Most macho managers are stimulus junkies.

The Macho Manager's Strategies

The second part of the macho manager's package of tricks are tried and true strategies that can be invoked at the drop of a hat.

1. *Create a crisis.* If you need a crisis, just call a macho manager; he will make one, find one, or buy one (another make or buy decision). People who can handle crises are openly or secretly admired, even when the crisis is a smoke screen. The macho manager's motivation is job justification, building up an impression of indispensability: "What would you do without me?" These staged events skillfully cause delays and waste resources. After having orchestrated the crisis, the macho manager walks in, guns blazing, and single-handedly rescues everyone while refusing help from bystanders.

2. *Don't share any power.* When you provide subordinates with information or give them authority, you are losing some control and power. The macho manager wants to build more power, not disseminate what he or she has. Dumping tasks on people without giving them authority is the preferred strategy for keeping it all.

3. *Create myths.* This is a fun activity that is devastating in its debilitating impact. Think of the myths that macho managers have perpetrated: "Personnel is a soft function," "Creativity is uncontrollable and only useful in R&D," "Workers just want money," or "Maybe I should take one of my other job offers."

4. *Don't postpone, "prepone" decisions.* Why bother postponing decisions until more information is gathered and key implementers are involved? A waste of time! The macho manager must act quickly and decisively. "Preponing" decisions (deciding immediately on the basis of one's favorite biases) is much quicker and cheaper and gives the impression of power, knowledge, and decisiveness.

5. *"Catastrophize."* This is a variation on the "Big Bang Theory of the Corporation." Create a "worst case," "scorched earth" scenario to scare people into accepting your position. If done objectively, this can be a useful minimax (minimizing maximum losses) approach. But in the hands of a macho manager it is used as an excuse to attack, dismiss people, or, most likely, put down a rising peer.

The Macho Manager's Cliché Catalog

The final phase of the macho manager's ritual is the art of slogan dropping. Because macho managers want to control, not create or constructively solve, they have an automatic, ready response system. To every call for inspired leadership, the macho manager has a proven, irrefutable, sanctified slogan or cliché. These utterances deftly divert any discussion from meaningful dialogue and chill the opposition. Here are a "dirty" half-dozen examples of these clichés, usually pronounced as the macho manager jumps on top of the table like Superman in a business suit.

1. *"The bottom line is profit."* This cliché, which carries as much weight as Motherhood, is usually mindlessly shouted after someone has brought up a moral or ethical concern.
2. *"Never up, never in."* This "truth" of golf is usually exclaimed as camouflage for a risky, unstudied, but self-benefiting strategy. Of course the corollary is, "Always over, never in!"
3. *"That's why you get the big bucks."* A variation of "it's all part of the job," this is used to berate a colleague who is disturbed about having missed his daughter's birthday because of a last-minute crisis caused by his boss's poor planning.
4. *"Time is money."* Was this mindless diversion ever preceded by the statement "Time is not money"?
5. *"No pain, no gain."* This means this is really going to hurt, but masochism is admired.
6. *"We need to run lean and mean."* This is a euphemism for the announcement in tomorrow's paper that 6,000 of the company's best and most loyal employees just got canned.

Macho managers do try, they do care—about themselves. After years of building this fierce, powerful image, they have begun to believe it themselves. The perception has become reality. Meanwhile, foreign competition wins, quality sags, and reactions to shifts in technology are tortoise-like. Short-run responses and quick fixes win out over long-term growth and development. So much time and energy, so many opportunities wasted!

The Antidote: The key is to pursue results, quality, and creative problem solving just as fiercely and passionately as macho managers pursue their own interests. Show objective strength.

Refuse to reward this self-serving behavior. Organizationally, reward loyalty, innovation, and thinking and acting in terms of the long run. If all else fails, after the macho manager has rattled off a string of favorite clichés and is wearing down, jump up and shout, "Remember the Alamo!" This has nothing to do with the conversation, of course, and therefore makes the point nicely and humorously.

Disease 3:   Praise Deprivation

Praise is the most powerful tool available to a manager, but most managers do not use it often enough. (Chapter 8 explains how to praise well.) Some managers are afraid to praise, some are embarrassed by it, some can't because they never learned how, others never received praise themselves. This begrudging attitude toward recognizing employees' efforts impairs the potential performance of the company. Many managers prefer to manage by using fear rather than praise. Fear can bring a quick burst of energy or a reluctant compliance, but in the long run it sows the seeds of defeat.

Myths About Praise

We don't praise enough. It's almost as if there were a finite number of compliments in the world and if we gave one, there would be only forty-three left. We use them so sparingly! This unfortunate behavior is caused by perpetuating some untruths about praise.

Myth 1.   *Performance should be perfect before anyone is allowed to celebrate.* Perfection is a debilitating concept that many managers have had drummed into them from an early age. There is always some room for improvement, so point out the deficiencies. If someone gets a 98 on a test, tell her she should have made 100. What a dreadful way to go through life! Stop looking for perfection and celebrate a really good showing. The celebration says "thanks, I care" and allows us to recharge our batteries.

Myth 2.   *Praise is overrated.* That's what people who don't give it say. Do you get more praise than you deserve? Neither do I. What we don't want, however, is begrudging praise. Too many managers give praise reluctantly, which diminishes its impact.

Myth 3.   *If I praise him, he'll want more money.* Actually, the opposite is true: People are more likely to demand more money when they don't get the credit they think they deserve. Some excellent managers have confessed to me in private that they are leaving the company because no one even said "thank you" or "great job" for something that took months of their time and was successfully completed. They aren't leaving for more money. They are departing to find more recognition.

Myth 4.   *That's what they're paid to do! I have better things to do than to slobber over people.* Since we all know that feedback helps us to know how we're doing, how do we justify this myth? Besides, if you respect me, you'll let me know.

Myth 5.   *Bosses don't need praise.* After all, they already get more money, more power, and more perks. The truth is that even bosses are real people who need to feel appreciated. It's not apple-polishing to give genuine thanks and positive feedback for things well done, especially if it helps you to do your job.

The Antidote: Because praise is the single most powerful tool at a manager's disposal, use it more. To be more effective, praise should be given—

- for any good performance;
- sincerely, not reluctantly;
- soon after the event;
- with a slight "positive" exaggeration;
- sometimes in private, sometimes in public, depending on the employee and the nature of the performance;
- as often as performance warrants it; and
- sometimes unconditionally, just to show you care.

A manager needs to build up a reservoir of pleasantness to draw on when an extra effort is needed for a rush project. When you've been working unexpectedly long hours, why not go the extra mile and thank the families that have been inconvenienced? You can become a hero or heroine so easily—in that most managers won't even think about those whose lives they disrupted. After the trouble and toil, how about some celebration?

Disease 4: Nearsightedness

Because our corporate leaders tend to think only of the short term, it is understandable that managers follow suit. Seeing distant things clearly has become impossible. Good managers get pirated away to other organizations. This mobility mania makes it more difficult to build loyalty. Dedication is not to the company, but to the profession. Of course our eyes play tricks on us at times, creating optical illusions that don't pan out the way we thought.

Nearsightedness is further fueled by our measurement and reward systems and the uncertainty of management's actions tomorrow. Managers fail to notice the self-imposed paradox: How can they demand dedication and loyalty when either party might sell out to the highest bidder in the morning? How can they ask for cooperation and team effort when the reward system reinforces selfishness? How can they develop people and products when both are measured according to next month's profits? Corporate short-term-itis breeds managerial nearsightedness.

The Antidote: The only way out of the malaise is to change selection, development and measurement, and reward systems throughout all levels of the organization. Following these suggestions would help:

1. Screen candidates more carefully.
2. Develop much more extensive training and indoctrination procedures.
3. Tie merit raises and bonuses for all employees to the accomplishment of long-term goals.
4. Set up a ten-year annuity for the CEO based on the company's position in ten years and not retrievable if he or she leaves before then.

5. Reward managers on the creative ideas of their subordinates to encourage development and cooperation instead of idea stealing.
6. Tie some bonuses to company-wide long-range targets.
7. Broaden the skills of employees to promote flexibility and personal growth.

Disease 5:   Fad Management

The tendency to rally round the latest fad is widespread in American companies. From MBO to Zero-Based Budgeting to TA to quality circles, management is waiting with bated breath for the next quick fix. Fads can be divided into old fads, new fads, and old fads with new labels. For example, one relatively new fad is management by wandering around, which is really the old fad of "getting out in the field or down on the production floor to see what's happening" with a new label. Fads evoke a quick burst of exaggerated zeal. There is nothing inherently wrong with any of the faddish concepts mentioned. In fact, if made a permanent part of the organizational fabric, they would be beneficial. What's wrong is that these concepts are merely being used by managers for short-run manipulation.

Some top executive reads a book or article and says, "That's just what we need! See that it's implemented tomorrow!" with no regard for the people it will affect or the potential organizational fit. Then he wonders why the troops aren't enthusiastically accepting the new fad. There is nothing wrong with an executive or manager initiating a new idea. But, as an example of how distorted the process can become, I have witnessed managers being *ordered* to form a quality circle of their subordinates. Quality circles are designed to be voluntary! Autocratically imposed participation is usually doomed to failure because of the implementation problems. Besides, if an organization really understands and values the creative ideas of its people, it already has some participative programs in place. The lack of a mechanism to tap the ideas of employees suggests a philosophy that doesn't value the potential of its people. In such an atmosphere, very few fads provide help. When an autocratic decision is made that "we will all participate and we will enjoy it," the originator has either a warped sense of humor or no real understanding of the process.

The Antidote: Most times, everyone affected by a new gimmick should have a say in whether to adopt it. Otherwise, implementation becomes an all-out losing battle (assuming the hidden agenda isn't to find justifications for firing half the work force).

Disease 6: The MBA Syndrome

Increasing levels of formal education in the United States and elsewhere have made a master's degree as common in organizations as a bachelor's degree was thirty years ago. The MBA has become the standard "union card" to attaining a higher level in the company. As one of my executive MBA students confides, "It doesn't open doors, but it keeps some from shutting in my face." So the MBA has become a prerequisite to the executive suite in most large organizations. It is a "necessary," but not by itself "sufficient," key for aspiring executives.

Further education is almost always desirable, and I should make it "perfectly clear" that I am in favor of graduate education in general and the MBA in particular. So what's the harm? Although there are many benefits to the individual and organization from graduate education, the harm is in—

- the distribution of what graduate business students are taught;
- how they are taught to think of themselves and others; and
- increasing mobility and decreasing loyalty.

The MBA is a Master of Business Administration. As such, each accredited MBA program, monitored by the American Assembly of Collegiate Schools of Business (AACSB), has to offer a wide range of required business courses. MBA students are supposed to get a little bit of everything. That's why, for example, a graduate is called a Master of Business Administration rather than a Master of Science in Human Resource Management. That seems OK. What's wrong with MBA students learning about all the functional areas so that when they become CEOs they will understand the entire business? That sounds seductively valid. But let's interject some truths here:

- All professors teach what they know. Most business professors are trained specialists who haven't studied the integrated nature of the entire business. They teach their specializations. One commonly taught course in the MBA program, Strategic Management/Business Policy, attempts to integrate the different functional areas. This one course is fighting the conditioning of years of practical experience and dozens of balkanized courses. How much integrated thinking will the student remember from this program?

• MBA students are, for the most part, learning "paper" management—quantitative techniques, financial techniques, statistical techniques, market research techniques—rather than how to communicate with, motivate, and manage people.

• Conditioning MBA students to think in terms of "paper management" often has a dehumanizing effect on their ultimate management style.

• There is inadequate attention paid to learning the "backbones" of the business—production/operations, motivating the work force, and sales.

• The rush to change the content of programs in response to AACSB dictates, such as the new push for integrating "ethics" and for "internationalizing" MBA curriculums, has often resulted in mere band-aid treatment of the topics, sometimes by professors who are just learning about the topics themselves.

There is a basic mismatch between what students are being taught and what they need to know. Most MBAs are receiving far too much training in the staff functions and are not given nearly enough courses in managing people and the line functions.

Second, how are they taught to think of themselves? Perhaps this elitism is more deadly than the knowledge mismatch. If you aren't extremely careful, you can create a situation in which MBA students believe that they are the only ones in the organization who can think. Of course, the more prestigious the university that grants the degree, the more severe the potential case of elitism. This education creates a gulf between those who manage (the MBAs) and those who do the core work. MBAs tend to overrate their own knowledge and abilities. We are training them to be data manipulators rather than managers.

In a poll of 480 CEOs reported in *Business Month,* it was a nearly unanimous view that MBAs were lacking in humility, humor, and humanity—all attributes valued by executives.[1]

Third, the MBA degree has a tendency to increase the holder's mobility and to decrease the sense of loyalty felt. Although not every MBA student is simultaneously working, many are. Often, the organization is paying for the MBA courses, and it is not unusual for some students to change companies soon after their organization finishes paying for their MBA.

The Antidote: As I have suggested throughout this section, the cure for the MBA syndrome is to shift the emphasis on the MBA curriculum from paper management to people management, from staff to line, and from intellectual games to the basics.

Healthy Organizations

In this chapter, I have presented six harmful diseases that have widely infected American managers and organizations. Whether it's managing by mind reading, applying macho management principles, reluctance to give credit, a short-term orientation, using fads like band-aids, or the MBA syndrome, the result is suboptimal performance. I have suggested that straight expectations, substance over style, celebration, a long-run perspective, employee involvement, and teaching the basics are the vaccines that will help bring health to our organizations and retard the "turning off" of our work force and customers.

Note

1. Michael E. McGill, "Attack of the Biz Kids," *Business Month* (December 1988), pp. 75–78.

Action Exercise

How prevalent are these managerial diseases in your own shop? After ranking the diseases below according to their measure in your work life, why not brainstorm some ways in which your group might band together to help change this behavior?

Rank Order	Managerial Disease	Possible Strategies for Change
_____	Management by mind reading	_____
_____	Macho management	_____
_____	Praise deprivation	_____
_____	Nearsightedness	_____
_____	Fad management	_____
_____	MBA syndrome	_____

Employee Diseases
of Excellence

Some of today's workers have turned Maslow's hierarchy of needs into a hierarchy of greeds!

Executives and managers aren't the only groups to exhibit diseases connected with the "I" of the beholder. We're all in this together. The final group that I will examine is the nonmanagerial employees. Just as selfishness can constrain organizational efforts at the top and middle levels, those less-than-famous people known as the doers can also restrict progress by their own unique efforts.

Most managers believe that unions bear much of the responsibility for the current poor quality and high cost of American products relative to those of our competitors. Managers who have to face strong unions every day and consumers who have to pay for the inefficiencies and disservice sometimes created by unions can attest to the problems they engender. But before I have some fun with the greed of these "doers," let me reiterate a point I made in the Preface. Employees don't vote for a union, they vote against management! Unions arise when management uses, abuses, and disenfranchises the work force. No employee in her right mind would want to pay checkoff dues for something she already has.

Historically, unions were the only avenue open to workers through which they could develop a power base to counteract management. Have some unions gone too far? Yes! Are some of them harming our competitiveness? Yes! Did management cause them to form? Yes! Many of our workers have been conditioned by management not to think, to do only what they are told, to put in their eight hours at the prevailing hourly rate, and then to go home. Management taught the workers that it wasn't *their* company, it was management's. Management wanted specialization. Now when workers act selfishly, refuse to do something that is not part of their narrow job description, and wait anxiously for the cue to leave work, we must ask ourselves who caused this behavior.

A second reason for the employee conflict encountered at work is the rising formal educational level of many American workers. This does not mean that they are *better* educated, as our increased illiteracy rates should show. But more education does bring with it an expectation of realizing self-worth. Today's workers expect to find not only a job but one in which they can use what they have learned. Most want personally fulfilling tasks. When they start out with a company, they often experience an unanticipated form of culture shock: Democracy is taught in the classroom; autocracy is practiced in the workplace. Many feel deceived. Their anger is then displaced in unproductive ways.

The following "fabulous five" employee diseases of excellence embody American workers' misdirected expectations and efforts. These avarices correspond (very roughly) to Maslow's hierarchy of needs.[1] Maslow's theory of a need hierarchy, which is explained more fully in Chapter 6, briefly states that people have five levels of needs (for survival, security, belonging, esteem, and self-actualization) and that these are generally pursued in that order. Once an individual satisfies a certain level of needs, the next level is activated.

The employee's hierarchy of greeds originates in the "I" of the beholder!

Disease 1: Money-Nucleosis

Workers aren't the only group who have internalized the greed for money; they're just very public about their demands and consequently the current scapegoats for the other organizational groups and their scams. Whether it's the UMW striking for more wages, a professional athlete holding out for $2.8 million a year, or farmers fighting to retain subsidies for *not* planting crops, the message is clear. Anyone with a gallows sense of humor and an awareness of the 1980s has deduced that many of our workers don't have needs, they have greeds. Management trained these workers to accept more money rather than enriched jobs. After watching professional CEOs take home $23 million in one year through salary, bonuses, perks, and stock options, the hunger and thirst of employees for more pay seem to have become insatiable. Observers could easily conclude that more Americans want more money for doing less work than any generation in the history of the world.

Higher pay for fewer hours with increased vacation time has helped to price American goods out of several markets world-wide. Is money the real issue? Yes and no. Certainly increasing everyone's standard of living is the aim of our economic system. Besides, making jobs meaningful is hard work. So management, already expending great amounts of time and energy on their games, opted to raise pay and keep the jobs boring. This easy way out has proved costly.

From the workers' viewpoint, money is often not the issue. But what fool would turn down more money? Also, task factors like control, responsibility, achievement, and personal growth are difficult to measure. So it becomes easier to push for more money or increased benefits because these increases can be measured. Yet recent polls have shown that most workers want meaningful jobs and most of them state that they do not have them.[2] These workers also admit to not working as hard as they used to or as hard as they could.

In our society, money represents a way of fulfilling many of our needs (for a further discussion of money as a motivator, see Chapter 6). Money, of course, can be used to provide such basic necessities as food, clothing, and shelter. Money can provide security through medical insurance, life insurance, and pensions. Money can provide a measure of achievement, serving as a scorecard for telling everyone how we are doing. Money can provide recognition and respect. Because money is so versatile and important in our society, it is no wonder that workers have developed a severe case of money-nucleosis. While some employees are working hard for more money, the same money, or even less money, for those who can get more money for less work, it's a very rational choice.

Disease 2:   The Sue-Bonic Plague

It's difficult to tell who started the current selfish trend toward suing at the drop of a hat. Perhaps the work force became greedy and lawyers appeared to answer the demand. Maybe, with so many lawyers graduating and looking for work, they have talked the citizenry into taking everyone to court. Whatever the cause, suffice it to say that the United States has many more lawyers per capita than most countries and, ironically, more crime.

In attempting to protect everyone's rights (a noble idea), our society has unwittingly encouraged employees to look to the law rather than to morality as the means of protecting their rights. Of course, abuses by those in power helped to bring about the current surge in legal actions. Yet the frivolous lawsuits that sometimes occur undermine the integrity of the system. These days, if I promote anyone, what do several of the employees who didn't get the promotion think of first? Sue. If I fire someone over the age of 45? This "sue first, acknowledge the truth later" mentality is destructive to both sides. Certainly, at least part of the higher cost of products and services is due to the burgeoning staffs hired to process and deal with legal problems. Perhaps even more important is the reduction of risk taking by companies and middle management alike as a response to potential legal liabilities. On the flip side, the avalanche of antidiscrimination legislation has built up an abundance of legal protection for employees, lessening the need for organized labor.

Disease 3:   Social Scurvy

The employee's need to be part of the group, which never was the most popular need in our society, has been replaced by self-aggrandizement and self-protection. The concept of loyalty has been dying a slow death. Of course this didn't occur in a vacuum. Organizations have used and abused employees for decades. The acquisitions, reorganizations, belt tightenings, and downsizings are polite euphemisms for mass dismissals. For much of the American work force, loyalty is a dinosaur. Companies have taught individuals to be equally expedient, and so manipulation for personal goals runs rampant. This phenomenon is exemplified by the professional athlete who holds out for more money, with little regard for team progress and unity. Just like the referee, however, we see the second punch thrown. The battle cry of both management and labor has become: "Ask not what you can do for the team, ask what the team can do for you!"

Disease 4: Ego-Addiction

Employees at all levels have developed into stimulus and ego junkies. The malady that afflicts them is characterized by job titles, perks, promotions, and pay. Status is dictated not by what one has done but by windows, carpets, desks, and the size of offices. A colleague told me that I must have great power in the business school because I had the largest desk and the smallest computer. I had not thought of it in those terms, but it was interesting that others did. It has become imperative to be materially and visibly more successful than other members of the so-called team.

In our society, being aggressive and ambitious can lead to sabotaging teammates, taking sole credit for what was done by several, and substituting selfish pursuits for group goals. Why not? That's the way the organizational reward system is usually structured. In fact, selfishness is such an ingrained part of the culture of some companies that actually caring about others is tantamount to being issued a do-it-yourself Joan of Arc kit.

Disease 5: Staff-Actualization

The top of the employee greed hierarchy is occupied by an ailment known as staff-actualization. Here, specialization, power, and self-interest reach their zenith. Some workers seem to find their true fulfillment in creating roadblocks, sabotaging schedules, building empires, raising costs, diminishing quality, and turning off customers. Being a specialist on the upper half of the left ear has become lucrative. Never mind the integration of the left ear (workers) with the rest of the body (corporation). Just concentrate on convincing the company that you need two assistants, one for the upper right corner of the ear and one for the upper left corner. Each of them will, in time, need two assistants, ad nauseam.

A Summary of Employee Greeds

Commitment, loyalty, teamwork, pride, and quality have become endangered species. When was the last time you received great service, the kind you want to brag about and share with others? Anyone who frequents the best U.S. corporations or has spent time in places like Japan can attest to what quality and service should be. A full-service gas station should be just that. Check everything, clean what you can, and then go out into the street and hold traffic so the customer can easily pull out.

People aren't born greedy. They are conditioned to be that way. Corporate executives, managers, and workers have all contributed to the sorry state of affairs we have reached. No one is to blame and no one is blameless. Short-run profits and poor measurement and reward systems lie at the heart of the matter. Why think in terms of the long run when the rewards go to those who think only of the short run? Why be team-oriented when individualism is what pays? Why treat customers with care when you yourself are treated with disdain and are repeatedly told that you just work there?

The issue that faces all Americans is how this destructive trend can be reversed. It should start with management revising its reward system so that it will be consistent with the corporate mission. Wouldn't it be refreshing if more companies rewarded on the basis of performance instead of according to position? Rewarded people who planned for the long run? Rewarded loyalty, commitment, team efforts? If we did, maybe we could reward the customer with value and create a positive, consistent team culture.

In *Megatrends*, John Naisbitt suggested that the United States, like it or not, is shifting from isolation and a national economy to becoming part of a global economy.[3] Consequently, we are only one player among a group of economically strong countries and regions, not the world's only dominant force as we were before. The time has come to reissue the call "United we stand, divided we fall!"

Notes

1. See Abraham Maslow, "A Theory of Human Motivation," *Psychological Review*, Vol. 50 (1943), pp. 370–396.
2. For example, see James F. Bracher, "New Breed of Worker Shakes Up Old Policies," *National Business Employment Weekly* (March 28, 1982), pp. 17–19.
3. John Naisbitt, *Megatrends* (New York: Warner Books, 1984).

Action Exercise

Which of these employee diseases do your subordinates exhibit? After ranking the diseases as they pertain to your people, try to identify the strategy that might be most helpful in shifting the emphasis to more constructive goals. And remember, employee diseases, like corporate and managerial maladies, may deserve space on the bulletin board in the appropriate situation.

Rank Order	*Employee Disease*	*Possible Change Strategy*
_____	Money-nucleosis	_____
		_____
_____	Sue-bonic plague	_____
		_____
_____	Social scurvy	_____
		_____
_____	Ego-addiction	_____
		_____
_____	Staff-actualization	_____
		_____

PART

Two

Managing Payoffs to Get Maximum Effort

Motivation is in the "I" of the beholder.

orses can sense the tranquillity or urgency of the rider. It is the rider who wants to get somewhere. The rider is the one who must be motivated first. The horse will usually respond to the rewards and discipline that the rider administers. However, when the amount of water offered is so small that it doesn't quench the thirst, or when the promised water turns out to be a mirage, trust is broken between rider and horse.

Different horses respond to different rewards. What should you use to reward the horse? Carrots? Apples? Sugar? Affection? If only horses could talk, we could ask them. Then again, employees can talk but some managers don't bother to discuss potential rewards and discipline with them even so.

Most behavior is goal-oriented. People are motivated or energized when they have a desire to accomplish a particular goal. Some targets are determined consciously, and others, unconsciously. People are not always clear why they do what they do. This part of the book addresses the "basics" of motivation, which many managers think they know but often in fact never learned properly. Athletic teams know that technique and execution of the basics win games. That's why even the professionals review and practice the basics every year before moving on to more complicated tactics. The purpose of this section is to explain how

47

a manager can understand, predict, change, or maintain the behavior of most employees so that organizational goals are voluntarily achieved. This section covers the basics of motivation, rewards, discipline, and praise.

If all employees wanted the same things, management would be a cinch. Just provide what they want in exchange for accomplishing the organizational goals. But first the manager has to discover what it is the employees want and then discern whether it is within his power to satisfy these needs. As you can see, when you have twenty subordinates each of whom wants slightly different things, the task gets harder.

Generally, there are two basic approaches to understanding how to manage people at work. The first approach concentrates on trying to comprehend human motives. The second approach focuses on the "process" of motivation and the resulting observable behaviors. Both approaches should be understood and integrated into the successful management of people.

Perspective 1: Understanding How Motivation Occurs

The first explanation of behavior on the job concentrates on the "process" of motivation and tries to answer the question "*How* does the process of motivation occur?" This approach begins with observable behavior as the key, utilizes the management of consequences to change behavior, and then moves to such issues as expectations and fairness. Managing consequences is the more practical route to understanding what to do as a manager. This approach explains how people choose various behaviors to achieve goals and how they evaluate the fairness of the rewards they get. The role of reinforcement theory is to explain the management of those rewards as they cause behavior to change or remain the same.

Perspective 2: Understanding What Motivates

The second approach utilizes the "need" theories of motivation to try to answer the question "*What* motivates people?" This view assumes that behavior at any moment is determined by the need with the greatest current strength and that a manager can study and predict these needs. Need theorists are helpful in explaining which needs may be operating. (These theories are explained in more detail in Chapter 6.) For example, if an employee is making enough money to pay for such necessities as a place to live and food to eat, and also has the promise of a regular job, then "unfilled" needs like social needs or the need for respect may be operative. This approach is useful and will be explored further in this section, but our understanding of the internal thought processes of human beings is rudimentary and, therefore, so is our ability to accurately predict any one individual's behavior. To further complicate matters, different people, groups, and cultures have been shown to value needs differently. Generalizing is risky business. Understanding needs can be useful in helping a manager to make an educated guess as to what an employee is pursuing. But in the present state of our psychological knowledge, it will be just an educated guess.

It is important nevertheless to make the effort to unravel what is going on with each of your people. Even if you are wrong, they will usually appreciate your effort and you can gain more insight for your next try.

This section of the book examines rewards and discipline, how to choose suitable and fair rewards, when to reward, how to praise, and how to set up a behavioral trust and change program. This information must be understood before trying to deal with the more difficult people.

Action Exercise

For it to be helpful, it is important that you relate the information in this book to your own personal situations. Before you read the chapters in this section, take a few minutes and jot down your current three most significant human performance problems and how you have been dealing with the employees causing these problems. (If you are not currently managing people directly, make use of problems with peers, bosses, family members, or friends.)

Problem 1: My most significant people problem is: _____

_____

_____

    How have you been handling this problem?

       1. _____

       2. _____

       3. _____

Problem 2: My next most significant people problem is: _____

_____

_____

    How have you been handling this problem?

       1. _____

       2. _____

       3. _____

Problem 3: Another people problem I am experiencing is: _____

_____

_____

    How have you been handling this problem?

       1. _____

       2. _____

       3. _____

The Art of
Motivating Employees

When your people are all moving in the wrong direction, for goodness' sake, don't motivate them!

n my experience, the single most useful and powerful tool for changing or maintaining behavior at work is the art of managing rewards and punishments. Oversimplified, this concept can be summed up in six words: *Behavior is determined by the consequences.* Each of us tries to maximize our pleasure and minimize our pain. At any moment, we do what we perceive will be best for us. In this light, people who do not do what we want them to do are merely dancing to the beat of a different drummer. Different strokes for different folks. Workers behave according to their perceptions of the available payoffs for different actions.

The founder of this approach, B. F. Skinner, states essentially that people tend to repeat behavior that is rewarded, avoid behavior that is punished, and drop or forget behavior that produces neither.[1] If the payoff for an action is pleasing to the worker, there is a greater chance that the worker will repeat that action. In this context, the manager doesn't so much manage people as manage the structure of the situation. The manager decides what payoffs will accompany which particular actions. The employee chooses among the options available and acts. The employee manages the employee.

Focusing on the management of consequences in the organizational environment has been called Organizational Behavior Modification by Fred Luthans.[2] O.B. Mod. is a fancy name for an organizational program that sets goals, monitors the work behavior, and applies consequences to elicit the behavior the manager considers desirable. (A formal organizational program for changing and maintaining behavior will be explored in Chapter 9.)

It is the manager's job to decide what work behavior is "desirable" and to choose and arrange the consequences for actions and nonactions. The employee will then decide—

- whether the payoffs are attractive or unattractive;
- what the strength of the consequence is;
- how much effort is needed versus the attractiveness of the payoff; and
- how to behave given the perceived available options.

Whether managers want to or not, they are continually shaping worker behavior by their actions, reactions, or lack of actions. Whether advertently or inadvertently, managers are constantly strengthening some worker behaviors and weakening others. For example, one often-overlooked consequence is simply recognizing the presence of someone. Saying "hello" or not saying "hello" may be inadvertent at times, but it can be perceived as pleasant or unpleasant depending on the importance of this amenity to a particular employee. It is not unheard of for an employee to walk away mumbling, "Now I wonder what she meant by saying hello in that tone of voice" or "Why didn't he even look up when passing me in the hall?"

Because managers must, as part of their job, arrange consequences to achieve organizational goals, O.B. Mod. suggests that it be done skillfully and systematically. Start by asking yourself why you want to change a certain subordinate's behavior. Is the behavior in question specifically related to performance of the task? Let's face it, sometimes a manager just doesn't like the behavior personally. Be careful here. Don't use up your energy, influence, and credibility on pet peeves. If, on the other hand, the behavior is directly related to performance, you will be attempting to achieve organizational objectives when you try to (1) increase what you perceive as desirable work behavior, and (2) decrease what you perceive as undesirable work behavior. You must first clearly identify the desired behavior. Next you must clearly understand the options or strategies available to you for eliciting that behavior.

The Four Basic Behavior Change Strategies

What are the options available to a manager for modifying or maintaining an employee's behavior? Most managers are accustomed to thinking that there are only two possible approaches to motivating an employee to action—rewarding or punishing. However, there are two distinct ways to reward and two separate ways to punish.

Two Ways to Reward

When I ask managers to explain the process of rewarding, they typically describe rewarding as giving an employee something pleasant. This is a reasonable explanation, but there are two specific problems with its application.

First of all, giving an employee something pleasant is not the only way to reward. You are also rewarding (making life more pleasant) when you take something away that the employee dislikes. So, initially, the manager who has decided on some desirable work behavior has two basic options for trying to strengthen that behavior: Add a consequence that the employee finds pleasant, or take away a consequence that the employee finds unpleasant. In either case, the manager has enhanced the work life of the employee in exchange for some behavior the manager finds desirable.

The second important point about rewards (Ah, there's the rub!) is that pleasantness is determined not by the manager's perception but by the employee's. The manager is guessing, using his knowledge about needs and the specific worker to choose a consequence that he believes will be pleasant to the worker. Here is where the frustration often occurs. Just because a manager likes something doesn't mean that his employee will perceive it as pleasant. Managers usually choose what they would want and assume their employees would want it also. But if an employee does not value the same thing, the consequence will not be seen as pleasant. And when the employee reacts negatively to the proposal made, it attacks the value system of the manager. "What do you mean you don't like what I like? What's wrong with what I like?" In this situation, the manager often gets angry with the employee. Let me make an analogy to clarify this sequence. If you had a bunch of keys on your key chain and you walked up to a locked door, you would try a key, right? And if the first key failed to unlock the door, you would try a second key. So why is it that so many managers, when faced with a reluctant employee and a bunch of keys (consequences), blame the lock? Why not just try another key? This employee has a different need. Let me use an example to illustrate the point.

Between a Rock and a Hard Place

A manufacturing vice president wants to reward one of her best performers. There is an opening for plant manager of operations in Cleveland. The vice president gets the promotion for the subordinate and then calls him in to announce the promotion with great glee, thinking she is rewarding him. But the possibilities are numerous. He may not want to live in a big city. He may not want to leave his family and friends. His children may be in a critical year in school. He may not even want more responsibility. His wife may have a job that she doesn't want to leave. If he turns down the promotion, what does the vice president think? She may question his loyalty; feel angry that her efforts have been wasted; think that the employee is ungrateful; begin to question his drive and ambition; feel that his values are all askew. This process helps the vice president to preserve her own value system. But she is blaming the lock! The subordinate may be just as hardworking and as capable as she is. The vice-president simply miscalculated the importance of the move from the subordinate's perspective.

How can you tell whether a particular consequence is actually desirable? First, use your understanding of human behavior and of the particular employee to make an educated guess as to what to use. (I explore the choosing of rewards more thoroughly in Chapter 6.) But realize that it is merely an educated guess! The only way to determine for sure whether something is seen as a reward is to apply or remove the consequence and monitor the subordinate's behavior. If the desired behavior occurs more often, you can assume that the payoff was pleasant. If, on the other hand, you try to reward someone and the desirable behavior does not increase, you can be sure that a reward has not occurred. It would be incorrect to say that you rewarded an employee but he didn't respond. The truth is you never rewarded him! You wanted to, tried to, intended to, but that is not what went down. If the desired behavior did not increase, the possibilities are as follows:

1. The payoff was not seen as pleasant or rewarding.
2. The consequence was pleasant, but not strong enough to elicit the behavior desired.
3. The employee tried but could not do it.

Regarding the strength of the consequence, there is a great difference between my offering you ten dollars to get me a soft drink and offering you ten dollars to work for me for a whole week!

The next important point regarding attempts to reward is that the manager should apply the consequence as soon after the desired behavior as practical. A time lag between the behavior and the consequence can distort the direct connection. For example, suppose that a subordinate does a great job on a project. A week later this employee goes to the boss and mildly threatens to leave if he cannot get a raise because he has had a more lucrative offer elsewhere. If the manager gives him the raise and compliments him on the project, what is he reinforcing? Good reports or threats? To complicate matters further, the employee may have said some things at the office party last night and wonders whether his remarks are the real issue. Whenver possible, reward the employee immediately after he has exhibited the behavior you want.

Another example is provided by the monthly paycheck. What does a once-a-month paycheck reinforce? The pay may or may not modify my behavior. It may only suggest that I have to do a minimum of work to continue to receive it, in which case the paycheck does not motivate my hourly behavior. Although it would be impractical in most cases, if compensation were given immediately after the desired behavior, it would be more effective as a motivator. If you are skeptical about my remarks on pay, consider the following example.

Instant Cash

Imagine that your boss walked around with his pockets stuffed with thousand-dollar bills. Any time he saw the behavior he wanted to encourage, he would simply hand the worker a thousand dollars. In this case, the connection between the money and the desired behavior would be dramatically clear. Workers for whom money was important would get on board with the desired behavior and collect some thousand-dollar bills. Those who felt insulted by the process would choose not to play. Most people, I suspect, would gladly play! The sooner the consequence came after the desired behavior and the more intense the consequence was, the more effective it would be. This example may seem farfetched, but I have heard from a colleague who visited a factory in Korea in which this procedure is in fact being carried out on a more modest scale. Someone is paid to walk around and distribute money to employees who are exhibiting the desired behavior.

The last point to make about rewards is that the consequence must be made dependent upon the desired work behavior as defined by the manager. O.B. Mod. is an exchange process with clarity of consequences and freedom of choice. It is much like a cafeteria approach to managing employees. The manager will give the employee this if the employee does that; or the manager will take away this unpleasant task if the employee agrees to do more of what the manager considers desirable.

Let me briefly summarize what I have said about rewards. The manager must decide what is desirable and undesirable work behavior. Hopefully, this will be based on performance, not personal style. The manager can then attempt to reward either by adding a consequence he thinks is pleasant to the subordinate or by taking away something he perceives as unpleasant to the subordinate. The employee's perception of the consequence used will determine whether the action is rewarding. The employee will also determine *how* pleasant the consequence is (intensity). The consequence should be clearly linked to a particular performance-based behavior, and given or taken away as soon after the desired behavior as possible. A reward increases the probability that the behavior will be repeated.[3] The more pleasant the outcome, the more the behavior becomes etched,[4] and the greater the likelihood that the desired behavior will increase. You can only tell what happened after the fact. If the desired behavior increases, then a reward has taken place. But remember that the consequence may be only mildly desirable, and what is being asked of the employee may require too great an effort in relation to the consequence offered. If it doesn't turn out the way you intended, remember, why blame the lock? Try another key!

Two Ways to Punish

Managers often think of punishment (which most organizations camouflage under the term *discipline*) as doing something unpleasant to the subordinate. This is basically accurate, but there are two ways to punish just as there are two ways to reward. The manager can give the employee something the employee perceives as unpleasant, or he can take something pleasant away from the employee. Technically, punishment by adding occurs when the manager, in an attempt to decrease undesirable work behavior, adds a consequence the employee perceives as unpleasant, thus decreasing the probability that the undesirable behavior will be repeated. An example of this type of punishment occurs when a manager criticizes an employee for wasting his time bringing up ideas. If criticism is unpleasant to the worker, then the manager has probably succeeded in discouraging interruptions and the communication of ideas. Notice in this example that two types of behavior are being reduced at the same time, one of which is very beneficial to the organization. This is akin to asking your child to tell you the truth when he has done something wrong and then punishing him when he does. He may still exhibit the undesirable behavior, but he'll stop telling you about it. (My daddy didn't raise a dummy!)

Punishment by taking away works like this. The manager, in an attempt to reduce undesirable behavior, takes away something that is pleasant to the employee with the understanding that it will be returned when the employee's behavior changes. An example might be a manager taking away an employee's coffee break until he cleans up his unsafe work area. How difficult it is to tell whether the consequence is unpleasant will be clear from the following example.

Getting the Runaround

Suppose you are a lifeguard at a swimming pool and you see a child recklessly running around the pool. What do you do? At most pools, there are safety rules forbidding running, so perhaps you blow your whistle and yell at the child for running. What have you done? You don't know yet, but your intention was to punish the child. Let's see what he does. Suppose the child continues running. Obviously, yelling at him has not punished him. What next? Perhaps you blow your whistle again, call the child over, and make him sit by you for fifteen minutes. This is an attempt to punish by taking away his ability to swim and his freedom (time-out). Is this punishment? The only way you can tell is to wait until the fifteen minutes are up and see what he does next. Suppose the child starts running again? You, the lifeguard, then become upset, angry, and frustrated. You see, there are several possibilities built into this simple situation, any one of which could be operating. For example:

1. What if the child dislikes the water? After all, he wasn't in the water, he was running. He may not even know how to swim, or the chlorine may hurt his eyes. And you have punished him by taking away his ability to swim?

2. What if he had been in the water and was being picked on by some bullies? They thought their behavior was funny, but he thought he was going to drown. Finally, with his last ounce of energy he escaped and ran away. You, in your infinite wisdom, tell him to sit right next to you where it's dry and safe. Have you punished him?

3. What if he is looking for attention? You've certainly given it to him. You may even have added status and made him a hero. Now he can saunter back to his friends and say, "That's right! I'm bad! I'm not afraid of that lifeguard. Watch, I'll do it again!"

4. What if, as a manager in one of my seminars suggested, he'd been running to the bathroom? That possibility gets really interesting!

These possibilities should impress upon you the fact that you can't be sure what it is you've done until you see what happens. You can't assume that the actions are punishing to someone unless the undesirable behavior is reduced!

Punishment: The Eye of the Tiger!

Punishment is complex and controversial, but it is frequently used in companies. Punishment is used more frequently when managers do not have direct control over important work consequences, such as pay. On the bright side, some of our healthy behavior was acquired in a naturally punishing situation. Swimming right after eating or learning to ride a bike were instructive because nature is such a great, consistent, impartial punisher.[5]

In organizations, punishment should be used only when rewards have been exhausted and only for a few really significant behaviors. An attempt to punish is like drawing a line in the sand and warning someone not to step over that line. There are several points to consider. First, don't draw too many lines. Unnecessary lines just create confusion and frustration. Second, make sure the line is clear. When a line is fuzzy, employees will test to see where the boundaries really are. Don't get angry. The line just wasn't clear enough to them. Finally, punishment unleashes some forces that are best kept leashed. Some basic facts about punishment might include the following:

- Punishment is complex.
- Punishment is controversial.
- Punishment is often used.
- Punishment is occasionally useful.

In fact, for the first-line supervisors with little control over policies, rules, and significant rewards, punishment (or "discipline") is an available, practical tool for shaping employee behavior. A lot of the interpretation depends on how it is used. Punishment can be instructive and helpful when properly administered. Don't forget, the aim of punishment is *improvement*, not retribution.

On the downside, punishment usually results in the short-term suppression of a behavior and has some undesirable side effects. Remember, punishment does not remove the original cause of the behavior, so it will probably surface again, perhaps in another form. When people misbehave, there is a reason. Sometimes they just can't see the behavior as undesirable. Other common reasons for surprising behavior are as follows:

- To get attention
- To try to win power or control
- To disguise their fear regarding their lack of ability
- To get even with you for something you did

- Just to be creative and have fun with you
- Change

Punishing an employee often results in hard feelings, which can take the form of slowdowns, sabotage, games, or spreading unpleasant rumors. Another disadvantage is that because the manager is treating a symptom rather than the real cause of the employee's dissatisfaction, when the punishment stops, the behavior often returns in full strength. Interestingly, on rare occasions, employees may deliberately misbehave because they want to be dismissed. This can happen when an employee hates his work but either does not have the courage to quit or knows that if he quits, he can't collect unemployment benefits. Finally, punishment may cause the unpleasant experience to be focused on the manager as the cause, rather than on themselves. Workers may transfer responsibility for the action to the manager, even when they understand that they themselves were at fault. With all these negatives, why do managers go back to the well so often with punishment?

Skinner has suggested that punishment is used frequently because it reinforces the behavior of the manager.[6] The punisher is actually rewarded by the removal of an unpleasant consequence (the employee). Punishment also gives the manager a feeling of power and an opportunity to vent frustrations.

Although quick, convenient, and self-reinforcing, punishment is not the best choice for dealing with misbehavior because of its risks, the difficulty of predicting outcomes, and the fact that it often represents only a short-run suppression of the behavior, not an attack on the root cause.

Punishment Without Guilt

Well! If you're going to do it, at least get it right! Having cautioned you about the problems inherent in using punishment, but recognizing its occasional necessity and widespread use, perhaps the best I can aim for is to help you understand how to use it effectively. In order to punish effectively and remove most of the guilt associated with being the punisher, I suggest that you carefully adopt the following ten rules:[7]

Rule 1:   Use punishment sparingly and only when you are unable to get the desired behavior through either of the two reward strategies. Sometimes you are faced with an incorrigible employee and no significant reward power. But even here, use a combination of rewards and punishments rather than punishment alone.

Rule 2:   Be very clear about defining and communicating exactly what is desirable and undesirable work behavior. When you think it's clear, communicate it one more time and ask your employees to state what they understand it to be. Being clear is very important to reducing the manager's postpunishment guilt trip. Are you positive everyone understood it the way you intended it?

Rule 3:   Make sure the punishment is connected to a specific, observable, performance-related behavior. If the behavior you choose to punish is ambiguous, the effects of the punishment will be greatly reduced.

Rule 4:   Tell employees *why* the behavior is undesirable, *how* the behavior can be changed, and *what* the alternative behaviors are. I am amazed at how many times subordinates are honestly not aware of what their behavior was causing, or what they could be doing instead. Share; don't manage by mind reading.

Rule 5:   Make sure that the consequences of a particular behavior were clearly understood before you punish and that the employee knows that you mean what you say.

Rule 6:   Apply the punishment as immediately after the undesirable behavior as possible to decrease confusion and increase the effectiveness of the punishment. If you grab a hot electrical wire, the consequence is immediate. The cause and effect are clear. You avoid hot electrical wires, don't you!

Rule 7:   Make the punishment appropriate to the crime.

Some behaviors can cost lives. We can't afford to be timid with these. But don't use elephant guns on ants. Every time a killer is set loose in our society and a teenager caught with three marijuana cigarettes rots in jail, our criminal justice system is further eroded. Don't give cause for disbelief in the appropriateness of the organization's justice system.

Rule 8:   Apply the punishment consistently across your work force. You may like some employees better than others, but punishment must be impartial.

Rule 9:   Try to punish in private. The punishment should be enough without adding the double whammy of public embarrassment, which makes it hard for the employee to back down. Because immediacy is important, take the worker aside as soon as possible after the incident.

Rule 10:   Try not to follow punishment with a free reward. Consoling the employee later to show your concern and support is one thing. Consoling the employee soon after the undesirable behavior because you feel guilty is quite another. You may feel guilty disciplining someone you like, but if you console that person too quickly after the incident, you run the risk of ruining the effect. When you scold a child and then pick him up to console him, he learns that if he can just put up with a little discomfort he can get a lot of loving. This rule is particularly hard, but the better job you do, the more effective it will be. You need to show love. Just try to separate the two things in the mind of the employee.

The key to reducing guilt in punishment is doing what you can and should to make the process credible. When you must punish, these rules should help minimize the bad feelings. When the behavior, consequences, and reasons are believable and clear, it is the worker's choice, not yours. As one company is fond of saying, "We don't fire anyone around here. They fire them-selves!"

Summarizing the Strategies

The chart shown in Table 1 should provide a helpful review of the four behavior change strategies presented in this chapter. The strategies are placed side by side so that a visual comparison is possible.

The Art of Combining Strategies

Although I have stressed the strategies for changing and main-taining behavior separately in this chapter to make them easier to learn, these strategies can and often should be used in combina-

Table 1. Strategies for changing and maintaining behavior.

Action Taken by Manager (dependent upon a certain behavior)	Employee's Perception of Consequence	Manager's View of Result	Strategy
Adding a consequence (+)	Consequence is perceived as pleasant.	Increases desirable work behavior.	Rewarding by adding (positive reinforcement)
Taking away an existing consequence (−)	Consequence is perceived as unpleasant.	Increases desirable work behavior.	Rewarding by taking away
Adding a consequence (+)	Consequence is perceived as unpleasant.	Decreases undesirable work behavior.	Punishment by adding
Taking away an existing consequence (−)	Consequence is perceived as pleasant.	Decreases undesirable work behavior.	Punishment by taking away

tion. Combined strategies are useful when there is one desirable and one undesirable behavior that are basically incompatible. For example, consider the problem of an overly dependent subordinate. When the manager pays attention to this employee, she is often inadvertently reinforcing the dependency. A possible solution is to apply punishment by taking away in tandem with rewarding by adding (positive reinforcement). The manager could ignore the subordinate's attempts to continue being dependent by removing her usual attention until independent behavior was shown. When the subordinate finally exhibited independent behavior, the manager could then compliment that person.

Another frequently used combination is rewarding by adding and punishment by adding. When a subordinate's job requires careful and constant attention to the task, then attention and diversion are incompatible behaviors. They cannot both be present at the same time. If horseplay is diverting a subordinate, the manager could try to punish the horseplay while rewarding careful attention. Rewarding desirable behavior while punishing undesirable behavior is probably the most frequently used combination of strategies. If you are not currently using these, try them.

Notes

1. B. F. Skinner, *Science and Human Behavior* (New York: The Free Press, 1953), p. 35.
2. A thorough examination of the concept was first presented in Fred Luthans and Robert Kreitner, *Organizational Behavior Modification* (Glenview, Ill.: Scott Foresman, 1975).
3. E. L. Thorndike, *Animal Intelligence* (New York: Macmillan, 1911), p. 244.
4. Edward Lawler, *Motivation in Work Organizations* (Monterey, Calif.: Brooks/Cole Publishing Company, 1973), p. 44.
5. Albert Bandura, *Principles of Behavior Modification* (New York: Holt, Rinehart & Winston, 1969), p. 249. Bandura gives an excellent presentation of negative reinforcers in Chapter 5 of this work.
6. Skinner, *Science and Human Behavior*, p. 172.
7. These punishment strategies are an expansion and adaptation of thoughts that were originated by B. F. Skinner in *Science and Human Behavior*, pp. 182–193, and of Douglas McGregor, "Hot Stove Rules of Discipline," in G. Strauss and L. Sayles, eds., *Personnel: The Human Problems of Management* (Englewood Cliffs, N.J.: Prentice-Hall, 1980), p. 221.

Action Exercise

Turn your attention to your own employee problems. Try to ascertain the strategies that might be beneficial in each of your problem situations. Using the three problems that you identified in the Action Exercise at the end of the introduction to Part Two, check the lines below to decide which strategies you have been employing and which ones might be helpful to try. A manager often gets in the habit of utilizing one or two strategies and ignoring the other possibilities.

Which strategies have you been using?

Behavioral Change Strategies

	Rewarding by Adding	*Rewarding by Taking Away*	*Punishment by Adding*	*Punishment by Taking Away*
Problem 1	————	————	————	————
Problem 2	————	————	————	————
Problem 3	————	————	————	————

Which strategies might be worth trying?

Behavioral Change Strategies

	Rewarding by Adding	*Rewarding by Taking Away*	*Punishment by Adding*	*Punishment by Taking Away*
Problem 1	————	————	————	————
Problem 2	————	————	————	————
Problem 3	————	————	————	————

Which combination of strategies is most appropriate? ————————

Choosing Fair Rewards

Life isn't always fair, but this doesn't stop us from expecting it to be.

To complement your understanding of the process of rewarding and punishing, I give you three critical, additional concepts that must be addressed. Once you have chosen the basic strategies you want to employ to change or maintain behavior, you must—

- choose the consequences you believe will be pleasant or unpleasant to the subordinate;
- ensure that the potential rewards are perceived as fair; and
- decide what pattern you want to use to administer those rewards.

The goal of this chapter is to provide some helpful hints on choosing rewards and then to clarify the issue of perceived fairness. Chapter 7 will explore the issue of when and how often to apply potential reinforcers.

How to Choose the Right Rewards

You can't teach someone something if he or she doesn't want to learn. The other person can defeat you and remain ignorant if that is his choice. Many people don't want to learn about the needs of others. Maybe they don't really care. Maybe they are too busy. Perhaps they don't believe the theorists. What they want is one quick, easy plastic overlay to drop over an employee that will permit them to say, "Aha, that's what motivates him." Unfortunately, there is no quick, simple answer.

Maybe some day science will come up with a shot that will allow you to read people's minds. Until then, it will take some effort on your part. Understanding people's wants and needs is tough work, but choosing suitable potential rewards for your subordinates is an important area of behavior management that can lead to big payoffs. So, how should you decide what to offer an employee as a potential reward for exhibiting the desired behavior? As you learned from Chapter 5, you won't know what the employee's perception of the reward is until you monitor the resulting behavior. Does this mean that choosing a consequence is based on trial and error? It does. But the better your understanding of needs in general and of those of your employees in particular, the greater is the probability of your making a good choice. Several notable authors have constructed theories that provide valuable insights into the business of making the appropriate choice.

Maslow's Hierarchy of Needs

Motivation is the energizing of behavior to accomplish a goal that fulfills a need. One categorization of potential rewards is presented in Maslow's hierarchy of needs.[1] I have suggested to you that any employee's behavior is precipitated by the strongest current need. Maslow postulated that human needs (at least in the United States) are typically arranged in a hierarchy, and that certain needs remain strongest until they are substantially satisfied, at which point the next set of needs becomes operative. Maslow's hierarchical order is:

1. Physiological needs (food, water, sleep, clothing, shelter, and sex)
2. Safety needs (security from danger, threats, and deprivations)
3. Social needs (belonging, acceptance, love, and kinship)
4. Ego needs (achievement, recognition, autonomy, and status)
5. Self-actualization needs (fulfilling one's potential)

The unfilled needs are the motivators. For most people, the physiological needs are naturally the strongest, and remain so until they are met; but these needs must of course be satisfied over and over again.

Yet not everyone pursues needs in the order Maslow lists. Some people sacrifice their physiological needs in order to achieve a goal they consider more important. Buddhist monks have done so for thousands of years, and artists, musicians, and writers in our own society frequently do so. Others sacrifice their safety needs, like the teenage gang members who risk their lives in street warfare in order to belong. In general, however, Maslow's sequence of needs is probably applicable to most of the American work force. Although no two workers have exactly the same mixture and intensity of needs, the general progression seems appropriate, with the needs becoming more psychologically complex as one moves up the hierarchy. Let's first understand what American companies typically use to satisfy each of these need levels.

Physiological:	Pay
Safety/security:	Fringe benefits (pensions, medical insurance, dental insurance, life insurance, worker's compensation, disability payments) and seniority
Belonging/social:	Unions and informal work groups
Self-esteem/respect:	Status symbols (office, job title, perks), recognition, and influence
Self-actualization:	Task competency, growth, and achievement

Second, looking at the broad picture of people at work, need theory has some interesting implications. Most workers in the United States have their physiological and safety needs met, at least in good times. Food, clothing, and shelter are attainable for most. In addition, for those who are employed at regular nine-to-five jobs (though not for the self-employed), protection from the potential hazards of life is usually available through pensions, various types of medical insurance, and disability payments. Safety and security needs are thus met in large part, although they remain continually important, especially to some age groups in the work force. This means that while workers may still pursue more pay as a means of upgrading their basic and security needs, it is the needs for belonging, respect, and self-actualization, which are often unfilled, that serve as motivators. These psychological needs are harder to understand. In fact, managers are not nearly as proficient at managing respect and potential as they are at managing pay. Pay is simpler to use as a reward or punishment. The higher-level needs involve the following:

- Creating task challenges
- Creating opportunities for growth
- Sharing control through delegation
- Sharing ownership
- Building group and team identity
- Giving recognition
- Building trust and respect

Although the manager will be held accountable for performance, for the employees to be able to grow and to satisfy some of these higher-level needs, they must be free to experiment— and sometimes fail. It therefore takes a strong, secure manager to successfully manage higher-level needs.

Finally, on the individual level, need analysis can assist management in determining where an individual or group is clustered. If you know where your people are, you can use need theory to predict where they are going next. A true leader must find out what his people are pursuing so that he can help them to meet their needs in exchange for their helping him to reach his goals. The Chinese general Lao Tse was fond of saying, "When a true leader has done his job, fulfilled his aim, they will all say, 'We did it ourselves.' " In other words, the true leader is so skillful at understanding people and at getting things done that his followers aren't even aware of his impact. Understanding need theory can help you to make an educated choice regarding the desires of your employees.

When discussing needs, it is useful to remember that employees have many competing needs. The mixture, strength, and priority of the needs will vary among employees. Some employees are more attracted by security, others by money. These levels of attractiveness also change over time. But these differences do not mean that managers can't make some solid predictions about the main directions their employees are following.

The great cultural diversification of the U.S. work force is reflected in the wide variation in the needs and goals of employees. Asian-American workers, for instance, because of their cultural background, may be more motivated by social than by purely individual goals. In the Far East, the belonging/social need often dominates. The group is the main unit, and individuals frequently subjugate themselves willingly to the goals of the family, nation, or the company.

Variations in needs and goals also reflect age (or stage) differentials. As people mature, they usually feel a greater desire to satisfy the higher-level, more psychological needs. This can be attributed in part to the fact that they have already satisfied their basic needs for money and security, and in part to a growing desire for more meaningful pursuits in life. Then, at a still later point in life, depending on their health or finances, people may descend back down the hierarchy to where basic needs again become a dominant concern.

Variations on a Theme

A variation on Maslow's hierarchy theory, provided by L. B. Barnes, suggests that employees may first follow the physiological and security pattern but then jump to *any* of the remaining three types of needs.[2] Clayton P. Alderfer, for his part, has fused needs into three basic categories: existence, relatedness, and growth.[3] Existence needs are equivalent to the physiological and safety needs; relatedness needs include interpersonal safety needs (group membership), social needs, and interpersonal esteem needs; growth needs correspond to self-esteem and self-actualization. This ERG theory was developed by Alderfer to more accurately reflect the research findings of those who had conducted studies to test out Maslow's hierarchy in operation. Alderfer speculated that the less one set of needs was satisfied, the more desirable another set became. For example, if I cannot get my growth needs satisfied, then my relatedness needs may become more significant. This may help explain why many workers who are seeking meaningful work but not finding it have wound up pushing for more money.

Still other researchers have discussed needs without attempting to arrange them in any order. David McClelland believes that workers have needs for achievement, power, and affiliation, where one need tends to be dominant for each individual.[4] Classifying employees according to one of these three needs may give a manager new insights into his people. If, for instance, an employee has a strong need for power and the manager is instead providing an opportunity for affiliation, both parties could experience great frustration.

Herzberg: Two Factors to Consider

A theory both practical in its applications and broad in its implications for management is Frederick Herzberg's Two-Factor, or Motivation-Hygiene, theory, which sheds light on potential reinforcers.[5] Herzberg's theory concentrates more on the personal goals of a worker than on the underlying needs that activate them. Herzberg postulated that there were two distinct sets of factors operating on an employee at work. One set, referred to as hygiene factors, determined the degree of happiness or unhappiness experienced by an employee. These elements, which described the task "environment," were—

- company policies and administration;
- working conditions;
- interpersonal relationships;
- type of supervision; and
- salary, status, and security.

The second set of work factors, called satisfiers or motivators, were contained in the job itself, and were comprised of—

- recognition;
- responsibility;
- achievement;
- advancement and growth; and
- components of the job itself.

Thus, Herzberg provided managers with a list of ten factors that seemed to be important in reducing dissatisfaction and/or

creating satisfaction. These elements can help managers conceptualize where their employees are at present and what they might
be pursuing in the future. They can also suggest what is missing
from the employees' work life. For example, the manager might
be providing responsibility on the job and wondering what to
offer next. Herzberg provides several possibilities. Also, this
theory helps to explain what causes good performance (satisfiers)
and what does not normally affect performance but does, however, cause dissatisfaction or complaining (hygiene).

An Inside Job

A valuable source on the appropriateness of rewards is you! You
may want to start by examining what needs you personally have
filled lately. A study that I did covering both the private and
public sectors showed that everyone from the top of the organization down to the first-line supervisory level was pursuing
almost exactly the same goals. It was natural for each managerial
level to think that the level below it and the level above it were
somehow different in what they wanted. The evidence, however,
showed that they were similar. Start with what you want. (At the
same time, remember that any one individual may not be on the
same path.) If most of your people can be reached this way, you
can then concentrate on the remaining few who are different.
(Chapters 10 to 13 deal with these unusual people.)

From your daily experience with the people who work for
you, you should be able to guess which needs some of them are
trying to fill. Just keep in mind that people and circumstances
change over time. Fred may not have been concerned about
money six months ago, but that doesn't mean he isn't today. He
may have had some costly bills in the meantime. Try your best
guess. Remember, however, it won't work for every employee,
every time. If it doesn't elicit the behavior you want, don't blame
the lock. Try another key!

When in Doubt, Ask

The best information about your employees will usually come
from having frank discussions with them. Why not be straight
with them? It is a fact that managers are judged on how their

subordinates do. This is not a secret. Both parties know it. In a very real way, employees determine their bosses' success. Managers, on the other hand, have control over many consequences affecting their subordinates. Exchange meetings can give managers a chance to find out more fully what their subordinates want and need; determine how these things can be supplied; prescribe what performance is required in exchange; arrive at mutually beneficial goals; and make verbal or written contracts explaining what each party will do.

Many managers suggest that employees won't give them honest feedback. When employees hold back information, however, it is usually owing to some signal the manager has sent, either consciously or unconsciously. A sincere, nonthreatening exchange, though it may be "tested" by the employee, will usually lead to the sharing of important information.

The truth is that managers need a certain level of performance from their subordinates. And subordinates, of course, have unfilled needs that they are trying to satisfy. Talking about these is beneficial to both parties. Chapter 8 explores more fully the problems involved in personally communicating praise to reinforce performance. For now, just accept the fact that managers can choose to be silly, deceitful, or honest in their discussions with subordinates. Straight talk is preferable to games.

Table 2, listing job-related items in terms of their importance, is a useful tool for beginning to gather information about your employees' needs. Filling it out helps employees to think about what is really important to them. And reviewing this data gives you as manager some interesting possibilities for future rewards. If this information is gathered before the exchange meeting, you will have on hand some hard data as to where each of your employees is before the discussion takes place.

Table 3, listing the same items, provides valuable information about your subordinates' perceptions of what you could be providing as manager. Inaccurate perceptions ought to be set straight. When an employee perceives that you control potential rewards when you don't, the potential for conflict or resentment arises. Perhaps you can provide a little of one need and some of another. Brainstorm how you might be able to provide for needs in other ways. But whatever you decide, make sure that the

Table 2. What do you want from your job?

Please rate the job-related items listed below according to their importance to you.

Job-Related Item	Very Important	Somewhat Important	Unimportant
Accurate and timely feedback	_____	_____	_____
Appreciation for work well done	_____	_____	_____
Attention	_____	_____	_____
Autonomy (being left alone)	_____	_____	_____
Being treated fairly	_____	_____	_____
Challenging work	_____	_____	_____
Clear company policies	_____	_____	_____
Clear goals	_____	_____	_____
Control of my job	_____	_____	_____
Flexible job duties	_____	_____	_____
Good interpersonal relationships	_____	_____	_____
Good supervision	_____	_____	_____
Good working conditions	_____	_____	_____
Interesting work	_____	_____	_____
Job security	_____	_____	_____
Leisure time	_____	_____	_____
Opportunity for advancement	_____	_____	_____
Opportunity to learn and grow	_____	_____	_____
Participation in decisions	_____	_____	_____
Pay	_____	_____	_____

Job-Related Item	Very Important	Somewhat Important	Unim-portant
Praise	_____	_____	_____
Recognition	_____	_____	_____
Respect	_____	_____	_____
Responsibility	_____	_____	_____
Sharing information	_____	_____	_____
Teamwork	_____	_____	_____

Note: A variation might be to ask subordinates how much of each item they are currently receiving versus the amount they would like to receive. Also, you may want to have subordinates rank the items they checked as "very important" from most to least important.

desired performance and subsequent consequences are crystal clear.

It is unrealistic to expect to have great initial exchange meetings with every single employee. Some workers are hard-core "I don't care" types. They may have cared at one time, but over the years they have become tired, distrustful, and resigned to seeing no progress. Broken promises, missed opportunities, or unrealistic expectations may be souring some of these employees. They will, however, respond to some rewards and punishments if only to protect themselves. Someone approaching retirement may just want to keep things where they are. You may decide, after a few attempts, merely to maintain that person's behavior till she leaves. Being successful means reaching most people, not everyone. The crime is that a few employees are actively looking for challenges and not getting them. If you reach just a few of these and turn them on while turning around their work life, it's worth the effort.

Does Money Motivate?

A huge debate swirls around the use of money as a motivator. Money is complicated and misunderstood as a reward. Will money get people to do things? Yes, if properly administered!

Table 3. How much of each item could your boss provide if he wanted to?

Job-Related Item	Could Provide Much More	Could Provide a Little More	Is Providing All That Is Needed
Accurate and timely feedback	_____	_____	_____
Appreciation for work well done	_____	_____	_____
Attention	_____	_____	_____
Autonomy (being left alone)	_____	_____	_____
Being treated fairly	_____	_____	_____
Challenging work	_____	_____	_____
Clear company policies	_____	_____	_____
Clear goals	_____	_____	_____
Control over job	_____	_____	_____
Flexible job duties	_____	_____	_____
Good interpersonal relationships	_____	_____	_____
Good supervision	_____	_____	_____
Good working conditions	_____	_____	_____
Interesting work	_____	_____	_____
Job security	_____	_____	_____
Leisure time	_____	_____	_____
Opportunity for advancement	_____	_____	_____
Opportunity to learn and grow	_____	_____	_____
Participation in decisions	_____	_____	_____

Job-Related Item	Could Provide Much More	Could Provide a Little More	Is Providing All That Is Needed
Pay			
Praise			
Recognition			
Respect			
Responsibility			
Sharing information			
Teamwork			

Money has some interesting characteristics that muddy the waters when it's considered a reward. For example:

- Money can be an effective reinforcer.
- Money is not the only reinforcer.
- Money is more attractive to some people than to others.
- Money is a surrogate item, that is, it's used to buy other things.
- Money can be very necessary at times.
- Money is often used to measure achievement.
- Money can represent recognition.
- Money can buy security.
- Money can buy off-the-job satisfaction.
- Money matters to most people.

There are also these considerations. Interesting work, control of the job, and involvement may be more important than money to some workers, but because more challenging work often is not available, money takes on added significance. Then, even if an employee does have interesting work, he expects to be paid what he and the job are worth.

Managers often do not have control over money in the work situation. Sometimes the compensation structure is set in stone, dictated by company policies or union agreements. If you have control of money, use it as an incentive. If you don't control the purse strings, turn to other potential rewards. Workers want money, but they want a lot of other things too.

Rewarding Fairly

A discussion of money as a reinforcer ultimately leads to the question of fairness. Employees want to be paid what they are worth and paid for what they produce. Subordinates constantly judge the fairness of their pay against several barometers. First, is it fair considering the amount of effort that is required to do the job? If the effort needed is out of line with the monetary reward, the worker will make some kind of adjustment to make the result more equitable. This inequity happens in most "merit" compensation plans. I don't know what the pool of money is ahead of time. I don't know what my piece of the pool will be till after the year ends. I may work hard all year, spending hundreds more hours than my peers, only to find either that there is no pool this year or that my peers are getting 5 percent and I'm getting 6 percent. Under these conditions, of course, money doesn't motivate. Why bother?

Second, workers tend to measure their pay against that of their peers, considering their perception of the amount of effort each exerted. If employees perceive that they performed just as well as someone who received more money, they will be dissatisfied and adjust their effort, usually downward.

Finally, employees keep tabs on what workers in other organizations doing comparable jobs are receiving. If what the competition pays is far out of balance with what they are now getting, and options are available, they will leave. Remember, the good workers usually have other options. It's the poor workers who stay when pay is out of whack with what the industry as a whole offers.

As one final thought on pay, let me use myself as an example. As a professor of strategic management I have options. Demand exceeds supply for capable teachers and writers in colleges of business. In other words, if I'm above average, I have options. If my university gives raises that are smaller than those given by other institutions, it is only a matter of time before this imbalance becomes a goad to action. Now, suppose further that I love teaching and that the salary gap gets to be truly significant (big enough to overcome my natural tendency to inertia). I may quit and take a job teaching at another university. The bystanders say I am motivated by money. Not true! I am motivated by teaching. If I wasn't, I'd be in industry instead of in teaching and consulting. I love teaching. But I can teach in either setting and receive a significant increase to change institutions. Sooner or later, large pay discrepancies between companies in an industry cause some of the best people to migrate. How many good people can you afford to lose?

When Do Rewards Work?

A potential reward can be effective in increasing performance when—

- the employee highly values the potential reward;
- the employee believes that increased effort will result in the desired performance level;
- the employee trusts that the manager will come through with the promised reward;
- the employee has the ability to achieve the performance being requested;
- the employee believes that the performance is part of the job;
- the employee perceives the reward as being fair for the effort needed; or
- the employee perceives the reward as fair relative to what peers are receiving.[6]

Significant rewards, trust between the employee and manager, and fairness are the critical factors needed for the reward process to work well.

Rewards for Today's Employees

Some things stay the same. Other things change. Today's workers are arguably the best-fed, best-dressed, best-housed, best-paid, and best-educated workers in history.[7] They are more aware of themselves, of their world, of the promise of the good life, and of the fact that resources are limited. To turn on these employees, you might want to consider some of the following suggestions.[8]

Money. Next to a "fair" wage or salary for the job, good benefits are probably of greatest concern to employees. Making the benefits package more flexible, to dovetail with current employee needs, is becoming more and more important as a potential reward. Flexible benefits allow dual-career families to structure their benefits so as to ensure complete coverage while eliminating double payments by both workers. Even for single workers, designing their own benefits package has appeal because it gives them flexibility and "control." A second potential pay enticement is financial counseling. Any help that will allow employees to escape the grip of the IRS on their take-home pay and spendable income will be appreciated.

Nonmonetary Rewards. Work can overcome loneliness and serve as a means for developing pleasant social relationships and even good friendships. Declining family relationships make the workplace the opportune setting for the satisfaction of individual social needs and the self-esteem that comes from being accepted, respected, and recognized. For support and friendship to flourish in the work environment, however, there must be trust and openness. A second potential reward is the sharing of honest, accurate information. Employees typically complain about the lack of feedback regarding their job expectations, performance, and company vision and directions. Don't underestimate the power of being "included" in what's happening and having input into what will happen as a motivator. Finally, creating challenging tasks for employees may be the most significant action a manager can take. Creating opportunities for the utilization and development of skills that will improve performance is critical from both the employee's and the company's perspective.

Mutual Rewards. When you know your subordinates because you talk straight and listen well, you can choose more suitable rewards. You won't always be right on the first try, but you will be right more often than the manager who doesn't take the time to learn about his people. Use the appropriate theories, your own experience, and open discussions with subordinates to learn what consequences will be most effective in motivating them. If someone doesn't respond, don't blame the employee, blame the consequence.

Work should be a win-win, not a win-lose, situation. You can get what you need by getting your subordinates what they need. You can have mutually beneficial relationships with almost all your subordinates by understanding the "horse's point of view." Don't be afraid of trying. After all, look what you've got to win!

Notes

1. Abraham Maslow, "A Theory of Human Motivation," *Psychological Review*, Vol. 50 (1943), pp. 370–396.
2. L. B. Barnes, *Organizational Systems and Engineering Groups: A Study of Two Technical Groups in Industry* (Boston: Harvard Business School, Division of Research, 1960).
3. Clayton P. Alderfer, *Existence, and Relatedness, and Growth* (New York: The Free Press, 1972).
4. For example, see David C. McClelland, *The Achieving Society* (Princeton, N.J.: Van Nostrand, 1961); or David C. McClelland, *Power: The Inner Experience* (New York: Irvington, 1975).
5. Frederick Herzberg, "One More Time: How Do You Motivate Employees?" *Harvard Business Review* (January/February 1968), pp. 53–61.
6. These items are a distillation and simplification of the approach found in the Porter-Lawler model, for which see L. W. Porter and E. E. Lawler, *Managerial Attitudes and Performance* (Homewood, Ill.: Richard D. Irwin, 1968), p. 165.
7. Frank Levy, *Dollars and Dreams: The Changing American Income Distribution* (New York: W. W. Norton, 1988), pp. 128–129.
8. These ideas are adapted from Richard I. Henderson, "Designing a Reward System for Today's Employee," *Business* (July/August/September 1982), pp. 2–12.

Action Exercise

What potential rewards have you been using with your subordinates? What are some new possibilities that you thought of while reading this chapter and now want to try? Why not schedule some exchange meetings? (Before you hold the meetings, make sure you read Chapter 8 on how to communicate rewards through praise.)

Employee 1: What consequences have you been using? _____

_____

    What new consequences might you try? _____

_____

Employee 2: What consequences have you been using? _____

_____

    What new consequences might you try? _____

_____

Employee 3: What consequences have you been using? _____

_____

    What new consequences might you try? _____

_____

Action Exercise

Switching need frameworks, how would you classify each of your employees according to need for achievement, affiliation, or power?

Employee	*Need for Achievement*	*Need for Affiliation*	*Need for Power*
1. _____	_____	_____	_____
2. _____	_____	_____	_____
3. _____	_____	_____	_____
4. _____	_____	_____	_____
5. _____	_____	_____	_____
6. _____	_____	_____	_____
7. _____	_____	_____	_____
8. _____	_____	_____	_____

How could you provide for these needs on the job?

7

Picking a Payoff Pattern

Common sense isn't very common and often makes little sense!

(O) ne question about reinforcements that is often neglected by managers is *when* the payoff should be applied. The answer is easy. I've said earlier that to be most effective a consequence should be applied as immediately after a target behavior as possible. But the question of *how often* you should try to reward an employee is more complex and requires some explanation. There are five basic payoff patterns available to a manager who wants to reinforce certain behaviors. Each pattern (or schedule) has its own advantages and disadvantages. The first choice that has to be made is whether you want to try to reinforce the behavior every time it occurs or only periodically.

Providing Perpetual Payoffs

There are three situations in which it is appropriate to apply a consequence every time that a particular behavior is exhibited.[1] First, undesirable behavior should be punished whenever it occurs. In that only a few important behaviors should be classified as undesirable, and in that managers don't want employees misperceiving that an undesirable behavior is permissible because nothing happened as a result, it is best to try to punish whenever the behavior is exhibited.

Second, trying to reward a desirable behavior every time is appropriate either when an employee is learning a new task or when the behavior is so significant that it does not occur very often. Because rewarding every time encourages quick learning, continual reinforcement is suitable in this situation. A quick and direct relationship between behavior and rewards, coupled with the employee's expectation that the reward will occur again, makes rewarding every time a powerful teaching device. With respect to complicated tasks, the manager may want to start with only a piece of the behavior and reinforce little by little so as to "shape" the total behavior. For example, when a subordinate has trouble accepting responsibility, the manager should reinforce even a small instance in which the employee took charge. But where the task is large and therefore does not occur often (such as a management report), then the behavior warrants reinforcement whenever it happens.

The third example is less common. Here, owing to changes within the organization, a behavior that had previously been reinforced is now ignored (every time) to try to get rid of that behavior. This might occur, for example, when a company tries to change direction and shift the existing culture.

In the real world, trying to reward a behavior every time that it happens has many drawbacks:

- Some behaviors occur too often for continual reinforcement to be practical.
- The manager is frequently too busy to constantly monitor the desired behavior.
- Sometimes the behavior occurs when the manager is absent from the work area.
- If a manager uses the same reward for a long period of time, the consequence may lose its effectiveness.

After the desirable work behavior has been established, the manager usually needs to change to some pattern of periodic attention.

Providing Payoffs Periodically

Once learning or the extinction of a learned behavior has occurred and the employee has made a definite connection between the behavior and the rewards, the problem is to maintain what has been gained or, better yet, to improve upon it. Learning will become more permanent once the manager clearly establishes a periodic payoff pattern.[2]

Periodic payoff patterns can be conveniently divided into two categories: patterns based on time and patterns based on the number of desired behaviors.[3] The categories are either fixed or variable.

Fixed Categories

1. *Fixed time:* Reward the first available desired behavior after a set amount of time has elapsed. Repeat the pattern, with the same time interval transpiring, before reinforcement. For example, you might choose to walk through the office at 1 P.M. every day (twenty-four-hour interval), looking for the desired behavior to reinforce it. Notice that this fixed time pattern is very predictable and therefore may not be as effective as desired. But it may be useful in getting employees back from lunch on time. Another organizational example of a fixed time pattern might be the monthly payment of salaried employees. But notice that the paycheck arrives no matter what the immediate behavior is. That's why monthly paychecks are not very motivating. The employee's only concern is to do enough to keep them coming.

2. *Fixed number:* A predetermined number of behaviors is allowed to occur before the behavior is reinforced. For example, perhaps every fourth time that your assistant delivers the absentee report on time you try to reinforce her. The ratio chosen will usually depend on the seriousness of the behavior and the convenience of rewarding it. For example, a salesperson's landing a big account is significant enough that you will probably want to reinforce it as often as it occurs (ratio of 1:1). At other times, the behavior may be relatively minor and frequent, so that you can't always be available for reinforcement. Piecework pay is an example of a fixed number of one: The employee receives a certain amount of money for each item produced. This is actually a continual pattern.

The bottom line is that schedules based on a fixed number of behaviors before reinforcing generate a higher employee response level than schedules based on fixed time patterns. However, both types of fixed schedules produce a drop in the rate of desired behavior almost immediately after the reward is delivered because the responses in between are predictably not rewarded.[4]

Variable Categories

1. *Variable time:* The amount of time between attempts to reward is varied. For example, after one hour, you try to reward the first observable instance of the behavior you want to encourage. Next you wait one day, then one week, then 10 minutes, and so on. You are varying the time between attentions so that the employee is not sure when the next reward will occur. As you can probably tell, varying the pattern is more effective in maintaining the behavior. A variable time schedule of reinforcement is most appropriate for giving praise, attention, or any reward that can be based on visits.

2. *Variable number:* You can also vary the rewards according to the number of times that the desired behavior is exhibited. For example, try to reward the desired behavior the fourth time it occurs, then the second, then the twelfth, and so on. This is the type of payoff pattern that is involved in gambling.[5] You don't win every time; when you win varies. Consider playing a slot machine. It is programmed to pay off according to varying numbers of behaviors. If the machine paid off every fifth time a coin was inserted, the payoff would be predictable and the pattern would be easily learned. But when the payoff is virtually random, it is much more effective in maintaining the gambler's behavior. That's why people continue to place coins in the slot. They believe that there will be a payoff, but they aren't sure when. When a gambler is down to his last coin (bus fare back to the hotel), he places it in the machine and walks home. Psychologically, each coin (behavior) brings you closer to the next payoff!

A salesperson whose pay is based on commissions is also an example of a variable number pattern. A salesperson is a positive person who knows that someone will buy, but she does not know how many sales pitches it will take before a sale is made. If a door-to-door salesperson knew that every fifth person would buy, she wouldn't need to talk to the first four people. She could just stop at every fifth house.

A manager can, of course, combine several of these strategies. For example, base pay might be supplied on a fixed time pattern (every two weeks), while bonuses may be given at variable times. Combinations can add variety, suspense, and fun to the manager's task. For the employees, combinations encourage be-havioral choices.

Training Your Best Friend

Allow me to stretch a point, have some fun, and, with luck, provide a few insights along the way. Suppose that you wanted to train your dog to fetch the newspaper from wherever the delivery person throws it, bring it to the front door, drop it by the door, ring the doorbell, and shout, "Paper's here!" How would you do that? First, you have already identified the target behavior. Next, you would have to decide what might be reward-ing to your dog. A dog biscuit and some affection might work. You would begin the training by doing what Skinner calls "shap-ing" the behavior. Little by little, rewarding each time, you get the dog to see that you want him to find the newspaper, take it in his mouth, run back up to the house, drop it on the porch, ring the bell, and announce that the paper has arrived. Now, let's suppose that you have accomplished all this by repetition and by rewarding every piece of appropriate behavior. The dog is now ready!

Monday morning comes: The dog does his thing and brings you the paper. What do you do? Give the dog food, praise, and stroking! Tuesday morning comes: Same thing. Also for Wednes-day, Thursday, and Friday. Interesting! Who is trained? I could argue that the dog has trained you to supply food and affection on demand. Anyway, you have been continually rewarding the dog for every example of the desired behavior and the dog has come to expect it.

Let's start week 2. Monday morning: The dog does his trick, and you supply the goodies. Tuesday morning: Maybe you are sick in bed with the flu. What does the dog think? What's going on here? Bummer! Maybe the dog will try it again just to make sure. Wednesday morning: The dog brings the paper. You are feeling better and supply the goodies. Aha, says the dog, things may be back to normal. Thursday morning: The dog holds up his end of the bargain but you are away on business. Bummer again! The dog makes one more attempt on Friday, and you are back and provide the expected treats. The dog now is faced with a decision. A pattern seems to have developed. Why bring the paper on Tuesday and Thursday? Monday, Wednesday, and Friday are the days for rewards. Or better yet, as a manager in one of my seminars suggested, an employee would think, *There had better be three biscuits on Monday or I'm not playing!*

Profiling the Patterns

To summarize, the manager has many options when it comes to choosing a pattern of rewarding. Trying to supply something pleasant every time a behavior or piece of behavior is shown will bring the quickest learning, but unless the behavior is infrequent, a continual attempt to reward quickly becomes too cumbersome in the workplace. The manager will usually have to switch to another pattern. Varying the application of consequences will be more effective in maintaining the desired behavior. When an employee believes that the reward will come, but isn't sure exactly when, a strong relationship is established that will bring more of the desired behavior.

Notes

1. C. B. Ferster and B. F. Skinner, *Schedules of Reinforcement* (New York: Appleton-Century-Crofts, 1957).
2. B. M. Bass and J. A. Vaughn, *Training in Industry: The Management of Learning* (Belmont, Calif.: Wadsworth Publishing Company, 1966), p. 20.
3. While Ferster and Skinner in *Schedules of Reinforcement* identified thirteen types of intermittent reinforcement schedules, showing the great potential diversity, the four primary schedules I have cited here, which are sufficient for our use, were identified by Howard Rachling, *Introduction to Modern Behaviorism* (San Francisco: W. H. Freeman, 1970), pp. 79–85.
4. R. Beatty and C. Schneider, "A Case for Positive Reinforcement," *Business Horizons* (April 1975), pp. 60–61.
5. Beverly A. Potter, *Turning Around: The Behavioral Approach to Managing People* (New York: AMACOM, 1980), p. 18.

Action Exercise

Think about the major problems you identified at work. What patterns have you been using to try to reward these people? What patterns might be more effective? How predictable are your actions?

Where might each of the patterns be effective?

Fixed time? _____

Fixed number? _____

Variable time? _____

Variable number? _____

What is the biggest error you have been making?

_____

_____

How could you change this situation?

_____

_____

The Art of Praising: From Rare to Well Done

The purpose of any organization should be to create prophets through praise!

Giving your primary attention to those employees who "screw up" doesn't make much organizational sense, but it happens all the time. Why? Let's look at a screwup situation for a moment. There are two possibilities: Either the employee screwed up by accident or she did it on purpose. If it was an accident, then the employee is well aware that she made a mistake. Calmly make sure she understands what to do next time and leave it alone. She is already embarrassed, and making her nervous about the next time may well lead to more accidents.

If the employee screwed up on purpose, then she either wants your attention, delights in making you angry, or has a subconscious termination wish. Don't reinforce your employees' attention-getting attempts. Burst their balloon if they want to see you angry, and take whatever steps are necessary to grant their hidden desire to be fired.

Don't give your attention to the troublemakers or the accidents. Pay attention to your best performers. Why is it that most managers can't bring themselves to use their time to praise the good people? The truth is that praise, given in the right way for the right reasons at the right time, is the most powerful reward at a manager's disposal.

The Personal Balance of Payments

In Chapter 6, in discussing the fairness of rewards, I suggested that employees are constantly checking what they get against the effort it took and against what their peers are getting. The employees will be tracking what others do and how their managers react and will be keeping a running score on the balance in this account. This account might be labeled "the fairness account," "the appreciation account," or "the pleasantness account." Whatever the employee calls it, this account has a current balance of "I owe you's," "you owe me's," or "we're even's." The manager's actions are judged against the subordinate's expectations. The military service expression for this situation is, "What goes around comes around." You get what you give. It would appear that part of the reason we are currently experiencing a national balance of payments deficit is that we are managing from negative individual balances of payments.

When your people have worked particularly hard one week to help you reach a goal, the "fairness account" has been depleted and needs to be replenished. Write a letter. Send some flowers. Thank your employees' families for the inconveniences involved. Buy them dinner. *Learn to think of your subordinates as clients.* The best salespeople spend a lot of time and money remembering and servicing their clients. The real estate agent who never forgets my anniversary gets my leads. The car salesperson who sends me thank you's and notes is "maintaining service" to the client after the sale. If managers thought of their subordinates as customers, the employment contract as the purchase, and the need to continue to provide service for repeat purchases, the world of work would be a neat place in which to spend time. From a selfish point of view, when you do something nice for someone, that person will usually bend over backwards trying to return the favor. Balance the account!

Don't forget, managers are people too! Very few people get the praise they think they deserve, including your boss. Just because she has more salary, status, and influence than you have doesn't eliminate her need for appreciation. When your manager does something that helps you to do your job, thank her! Honest, timely feedback is not brownnosing. Subordinates are quick to take what they can get but slow to say thanks. Refill your account with your boss as well as with your subordinates. If your boss is miserly with praise, perhaps you can help build the kind of climate in which it is OK to give honest, positive feedback. Be the catalyst!

Producing Potent Praise

It doesn't take a genius to conclude that miscommunication is at the heart of most human problems. Managers spend most of their time either communicating or thinking about communications. Most communications go awry in the implementation phase. The sender knows what should be communicated, but sometimes doesn't bother (thus practicing Management By Mind Reading), or sends confusing, ambiguous messages either on purpose or subconsciously.

The three basic methods of communicating in the organizational setting are writing, telephone conversations, and face-to-face (or video conferencing) conversations. These three forms of communicating are in an increasing order of complexity. With written communication, only sight is involved and there is usually plenty of time to choose words carefully. On the telephone, the participants can hear the words and experience the tone of voice and inflexion. But in a face-to-face interaction, the receiver can see the body language and facial expressions in addition to hearing the words, tone of voice, and inflexion. For face-to-face communications to be effective, there must be agreement among the *style* of communication (inflexion and tone of voice), the *substance* of the communication (words), and the *silent* communications (body language and facial expressions).

When to Praise in Writing

Communicating in writing has both advantages and drawbacks. The good news is that writing—

- allows the sender plenty of time to compose the message carefully;
- acts as a permanent document to remind everyone of exactly what was said;

- allows mass communication to occur almost simultaneously; and
- covers great distances cheaply.

The bad news is that writing—

- is impersonal;
- does not permit immediate feedback; and
- can be used against you later.

Be prudent regarding what you put into writing. Unless a message calls for a carefully worded, lasting document for mass consumption, turn to another form of communication. The more memos, procedures, and policies you produce, the less they get read. On the other hand, a letter to Europe (or a telex) is much less expensive than a visit.

When to Phone In Your Praise

Remember the first time you heard your own voice on a tape recording? Wasn't that a shock? That lesson should guide your decision as to whether to use the telephone to communicate praise. Some people do not seem able to put any emotion into their voices when they speak. Your voice is all the recipient has to go by on the telephone.

Of course, the main advantage of communicating praise over the phone is the opportunity it gives for gaining immediate feedback. Also, some people find it easier to communicate when they can't see the other person. Telephone conversations can be revealing. The telephone can be a resource or an albatross. Use it wisely. Perhaps the use of a short phone call for immediacy followed by a meeting at the first available opportunity would make a desirable combination.

Communicating Praise Face-to-Face

Most praise should be given in person. But because face-to-face communications involve the complexity of words, voice inflexion, and body language, it takes great skill to transfer praise effectively. Whether you want to refer to praise as stroking, recognition, reinforcement, or engendering good feelings, there are three specific aspects of the transaction that must be understood. Substance, style, and silent messages must all be appropriate, both individually and in combination.

Substance Use and Abuse

Substance pertains to the central meaning or significance of the intended communication. As such, words are the prime substantive part of the attempted transfer of meaning. The words chosen to communicate praise are important from two distinct perspectives. First, how the manager phrases the intended compliment will influence the effectiveness of the praise. Second, even in a potentially effective phrasing, the choice of words will be more or less appealing to a particular subordinate.

There are two types of praise given in organizations: noncontingent praise—"You're such a friendly person" or "I like your suit!"—and contingent praise—"You did a great job on that report I asked for" or "Thanks, you arranged those supplies just the way I wanted them." Contingent praise is given for performance. The contingency is, "If you do what I want done, I will compliment you for it." In either case, the best strategy for the giver is to phrase it concisely, specifically, and sincerely and to relate it to performance where possible. Anything other than sincere, concise, specific praise is ineffective. For example, consider some of what managers try to pass off as praise:

Puzzling Praise: This kind of praise is too general or ambiguous, and usually leaves the recipient wondering what the manager really meant. Examples are "Not bad," "OK," or "Pretty good." This stuff rolls off one person's tongue and the other person's back. What happened to "Great presentation!" "Super report!" and "Excellent letter!"?

Phony Praise: Such praise is artificial because you give it not just to a specific subordinate but to perhaps 3,000 other "intimate" friends as

	well. An example is, "You're looking bright-eyed and bushy-tailed as ever today." The phoniness of these words is usually obvious from the bored inflexion accompanying them.
Public Praise:	This type of praise is used for effect almost exclusively in front of other people. An example occurs when a subordinate with whom you are having problems compliments you in front of your boss.
Put-Down Praise:	Here the compliment seems positive, but is actually a setup for the put-down. For example, "That was a great piece of market research you did. It's too bad you forgot to include the most important item." Or saying to an employee who prides himself on his creativity, "I'll have to hand it to you for conscientiousness."

The receiver of the compliment can also be responsible for ruining, deflecting, or refusing to acknowledge attempts to praise. Some people don't really feel good about themselves and therefore have great difficulty in accepting positive praise. You can help them to understand that you mean it, that they are worthy, and that the best response to praise is a simple "Thank you," no matter what the intent of the giver.

The second part of the substance of praise is to choose the words that will be most meaningful to a particular receiver. In other words, *pick the proper pathway to enhance acceptance and to be effective.* Subordinates exhibit many individual differences, and this dictates the necessity for taking a slightly different path to reach each person. To illustrate, consider the following three possibilities:

1. *Sensing.* Some people perceive the world in accordance with a preference for one of the five senses. For example, some people "see" the world and communicate by means of words that relate to sight. Try using sight words with them, as in "I *see* what you mean," or "I can *picture* your invention." Others "hear" the world and use auditory words in their discussions. With these

workers, say something like "That response was clear as a bell" or "Your answer sounded great" to put them at ease. Still other employees talk in terms of emotion. To them, "feeling" that they have performed well is important. Respond to them in their own language.

2. *External or internal focus.* Extroverts tend to expect praise. Give it to them; they thrive on it. Introverts are likely to be more skeptical about compliments. They need more time to consider what you say. Don't rush them. Also, because introverts are more apt to question praise, make sure you are very specific, not only about what you are complimenting them for but about why what they have done is important to attaining the organization's goals.

3. *Outline/detail.* Subordinates usually have a tendency to favor either the big picture or the details. For the "outline" employees, details are boring. Don't bother muddying their waters with too narrow an explanation. On the other hand, the "detail" people need to know the specifics. Fill it in for them, A to Z. (Just tell the outline people there was an alphabet, and they'll understand.)

If you choose your words carefully, depending on the particular employee you are trying to praise, you can greatly enhance the effectiveness of your communication.

Style: Delivering the Goods

Even when you choose your words carefully, there is still the possibility that your praise may be ineffective because of problems with the way you gave it. The inflexion and intonation can be at odds with the meaning. I am convinced that this is where most potentially effective communication breaks down. The manager knows how important praise is and knows what should be said but does not feel good about doing it. This reluctance is readily apparent in the way the message is delivered. Consider the following statement: "Mary, you did a dynamite job on this week's presentation!" Seems effective, doesn't it? But by this time the manager should have noticed that if Mary is a detail person, specifics need to be incorporated in any praise given. Also, when you read this statement to yourself, how do you read it? If you place the emphasis on the words "this week," you destroy the potentially pleasant impact of the rest. The manager can in this sneaky way remind the employee that past performances have not been great and that one presentation does not constitute a firm trend. Ugh! The manager might as well not have complimented her at all. Equally depressing is the reluctant tone of voice used when telling Mary the news. Musicians say you can hear a smile in a singer's voice. They're right!

Silent Messages

Finally, just as tone of voice and emphasis can dampen an otherwise effective message, so can body language. If the body language is not consistent with the words used, it sends an uneasy, perhaps subconscious message that all is not what it seems. What would the effect of the message to Mary be if the boss kept tapping his pencil or looking at his watch as he gave it? Look the employee straight in the eyes, smile, and give her the good news as if you meant it.

Roadblocks to Effective Praise

Besides mistakes in the substance, style, and silent language of the communication, there are two mistakes commonly made in communicating that are worth mentioning separately.

1. *Violating the Law of Verticality.* Have you ever noticed how some people are as brazen as bulls in a china shop while others are as meek as lambs? In a verbal exchange, it is unusual to see both people standing straight up, being equally assertive while respecting the rights and opinions of the other individual. Most times, one person is leaning into the other, who is leaning back. Neither person sees what we as bystanders see. As an example, how often have you heard someone say, "Well, I really gave it to him, didn't I?" Meanwhile, you were there at the meeting and did not walk away with this impression. On the opposite side, someone says, "Maybe I should have been more forceful," while your impression was that this person had acted like a bona fide graduate of the Attila the Hun Graduate School of Management.

In both situations, the individuals did not seem to have a good grasp of reality. Neither person was practicing the law of verticality—merely standing up straight, entitled to the space above, beside, and behind him. In the first instance, the person was leaning way back, yet thinking he was being assertive. In the second situation, the person was leaning way in, violating the other person's space, yet imagining that he was not being forceful enough. As Ben Bissell, a noted management consultant, has suggested, people have a natural tendency either to charge into the other person with an intimidating style, or to be meek and invite the other person to lean into them.[1] It is necessary for both parties to stand up straight for effective communication to occur. Managers must take care that when praise is given, it occurs in the context of a balanced exchange between two respectful adults.

2. *Getting Trapped by Implied Agreement.* There are multiple meanings to "yes" in any culture. In the United States, it can mean "yes, I hear you," "yes, I understand you," "yes, I agree with you," or "yes, and I'm going to follow through on that!" When you nod your head and mumble "uh-huh," the other person tends to assume that you agree with what he is saying. This can lead to your being quite surprised if later, the other party says you agreed to something you hadn't really thought about. When you announce that you actually disagreed, the other party rises in indignation to assail your turncoat behavior. If you are doing the communicating and the other person is nodding in agreement, the way to get past this trap is to ask him specifically whether he agrees with what you are saying. Be sensitive to your own behavior and clarify your position before you depart. Something as simple as, "Do you understand why I am so pleased with your work?" may prevent a possible disaster.

A Congruent Ending

As a final thought on communicating praise effectively, consider the importance of three variables: what you have experienced, what you are aware of, and your behavior. Carl Rogers was the first to analyze the need for congruence between experience, awareness, and intentions.[2] Sometimes the communication is ineffective because of inconsistencies between experience and awareness. You may be angry and showing anger to all within earshot, but denying that you are upset. Sometimes there is a difference between awareness (which is accurate) and what you communicate. Think about attending the worst office party of your life. Awareness says it was awful. But what do you say to the boss as you are leaving? If you say, "I had a great time," awareness and behavior intentions are inconsistent. But you don't have to choose between lying and offending. You could just say, "Thanks for all the work you put into this party," and mean it. Remember, deception is a trap that is all too easy to fall into unless we realize what a lot of trouble will be saved in the long run by communicating the truth. Do not, therefore, either overdo or underdo your praise. Find out how your subordinates like their steak and serve accordingly.

Notes

1. Ben Bissell, *How to Handle Difficult People* (Richmond, Va.: BenLu Enterprises, 1985).
2. Carl R. Rogers and F. J. Roethlisberger, "Barriers and Gateways to Communication," *Harvard Business Review*, Vol. 30, No. 4 (July-August 1952), pp. 28–34.

Action Exercise

Select three employees who have performed well on some task you have assigned them and who have not yet received recognition from you.

Employee 1: _____

Employee 2: _____

Employee 3: _____

Decide where, when, and how it would be most appropriate to recognize their contributions.

Employee 1:

   Where: _____   When: _____   How: _____

Employee 2:

   Where: _____   When: _____   How: _____

Employee 3:

   Where: _____   When: _____   How: _____

How can you specifically word your praise so that it will be most clear, effective, and meaningful to each of the three employees?

Employee 1: _____

_____

Employee 2: _____

_____

Employee 3: _____

_____

Write a thank-you note to some party indirectly involved in the performance (another manager, employee, spouse/family).

Action Exercise

It should be useful for you to take some time to categorize the tendencies of each of your subordinates. Do your best to determine their leanings. If you are unsure, wait and observe them, keeping in mind the elements listed below.

Employee	Sight/ Hearing/ Feeling	Extroversion/ Introversion	Ability to Outline/for Detail
1. _____	_____	_____	_____
2. _____	_____	_____	_____
3. _____	_____	_____	_____

Setting Up a Behavioral Trust and Change Program

One of Murphy's Laws: The biggest myth of management is that management actually exists.

eter Drucker once said that the bottleneck is always at the head of the bottle. This statement has great meaning in organizations because, as I have explained in Chapters 1 and 5, it is employees' perceptions regarding management that determine their behavior. Fairness, consistency, and clarity in management actions and demands are critical to employee acceptance and performance.

There are no cure-alls! That's why managers, like doctors, need to have a black bag filled with different possible solutions. If a manager uses only one approach to all problems, then whether the approach works or not is strictly a function of chance. If the variables are correct, the approach may be fruitful. If not, it will fail. Think about a doctor who carries only penicillin in his bag. When he stumbles across a man bleeding to death, a shot is not the answer. However, if he is lucky enough to face a patient with pneumonia, he succeeds and believes his method has proved correct. Pure chance! It is the same with management. If the manager has only one specific style that he can use to manage, then it is strictly chance when the style fits the employee. Fill up your bag! Learn to use many different styles depending on the needs of your subordinates. Have many different possible cures available.

One potential addition to your black bag is a behavioral trust and change program. How useful this program can be will depend on your individual situation. A formal program that is clear and consistent is often missing in the workplace. Although it is relatively inexpensive to set up and use and useful to varying degrees, a program for behavioral trust and change will be most advantageous when—

- past performance/reward links have been perceived by the employees as capricious;
- performance can be objectively measured;
- you have the capability of distributing significant potential rewards;
- "activity" has become the norm rather than "results";
- employees desire more choices;
- feedback has been insufficient; or
- employee creativity (new and better ways of doing things) can contribute to the accomplishment of organizational objectives.

The Steps in a Behavioral Trust and Change Program

A generic model of the items involved in a behavioral trust and change program is presented below.[1] It is generic because any successful process must be tailored to your own organization, people, situation, and needs. There are ten steps:

1. *Judge the fit.* Begin your efforts by analyzing your organization's realities and needs. If a behavioral trust and change program seems appropriate, consider the elements below but shape them to fit your own, unique setting.

2. *Build a success story.* Begin with a few jobs for which performance is easy to measure so that you can build up the credibility of the program in the eyes of employees. Be sure to identify who controls performance and reward accordingly. If a worker is dependent on the performance of someone else, use group incentives. Use individual incentives only when the worker is independent and has great control over the completion of the task.

3. *Choose the behavior you want.* Identify only specific, observable, performance-related behavior. Look at the task and distin-

guish the desirable, undesirable, and irrelevant behavior. Don't classify behavior as undesirable just because it doesn't suit you personally. Try to control your biases. If you are a stickler for a clean desk and I have a sloppy desk, don't assume I'm doing less work. When you see two employees talking, don't assume they are wasting time—they may be, they may not be. Yelling at them may decrease performance, especially if they are sharing a work problem. Even if they aren't, sometimes a break is beneficial. How are their results? You will have to wrestle with these possibilities in your own shop. Be objective. Keep your own behavior task-related!

4. *Monitor when, where, and how often the behavior occurs.* Some behavior happens on a particular day of the week or at a particular time of the day. Any time a consistent pattern is found, the behavior is not capricious. For example, an employee may be late to work every Tuesday morning. The explanation may be something as simple as that Tuesday is her day for being the driver of a car pool. Where the behavior occurs is important. It may be that the presence of another person or an environmental factor is the catalyst. People can be like chemicals that are harmless when separate but explosive when mixed. Check it out! Finally, find out how often the behavior is occurring. It may seem as if every time you check, Sam is absent from his desk, but it is possible that he is there at other times or that Jane is missing more often than Sam. Monitor and record the frequency of the behavior. This objectivity can help keep the egg off your face.

5. *Consider the present consequences of the behavior.* Remember, most people act in rational ways to maximize pleasure and/or minimize pain, as they perceive it. Maybe the consequence is not important to the employee. Perhaps the consequence is actually encouraging the behavior. Often we reward troublemakers with transfers to more desirable assignments just to get rid of them. Sometimes we give employees our attention when they misbehave. Analyze the situation. What does the employee want and how can she get it in this environment?

6. *Hold exchange meetings with your people.* The importance of these meetings and how they work have already been discussed in Chapter 6. Suffice it to say that you must share information, expectations, perceptions, and goals, and find reasonable, workable solutions that are mutually beneficial.

7. *Choose and communicate your strategies.* The exchange meetings should result in the formulation and establishment of the best strategies for behavioral change (rewards/punishments). Be positive and try to gain a clear understanding and commitment from each employee.

8. *Check the resulting behavior.* Output, quality, and defects should be carefully monitored, measured, and recorded. Some of the organizational measures already in place should provide information. Gather whatever is missing. Allow the employees to do some self-monitoring, which can provide valuable insight in itself. When an employee is forced to keep his own records, he will be much more aware of how he is doing against the agreed-upon targets. In addition, you can provide performance feedback that is not readily available to the employee.

9. *Deliver what you promised.* This is your chance to build trust by showing the employee and any interested observers what happens when someone performs well. Praise! Recognize! Give money! Strengthen good performances!

10. *Regroup.* Evaluate the results against the desired state of affairs and make the necessary changes or updates. Remember, as tasks, goals, or needs change, you will have to adjust the program accordingly. An old goal that has become unattainable because of changes in the environment but that is still being pursued can become terribly frustrating to the troops.

Trust comes to the manager who cares about the task and the people. A behavioral trust and change program is a straightforward agreement between the boss and his subordinates. It lays out the task-related behavior and the possibilities and consequences associated with each action. Find out what they need. Tell them what you need. Match up these needs with your capacity to deliver and let the employees choose. This clear, consistent contract gives the employees much more flexibility and freedom than Management By Mind Reading.

Note

1. These steps represent a revision of a set of concepts first introduced in the Behavioral Contingency Management Model found in Fred Luthans and Robert Kreitner, *Organizational Behavior Modification* (Glenview, Ill.: Scott Foresman, 1975), pp. 123–128, and expanded in Ken Matejka, *Handling Human Performance* (Englewood Cliffs, N.J.: Prentice-Hall, 1982), pp. 52–56.

Action Exercise
Behavioral Trust and Change Report Form

Task being examined: _____   Date: _____

Employee: _____

What are the three most desirable behaviors associated with this task?

    1. _____

    2. _____

    3. _____

How often have these behaviors been occurring?

____ Very often   ____ Fairly often   ____ Not often

Have you clearly communicated this perception to the employee?

____ Yes ____ No

What are the undesirable behaviors associated with this task?

    1. _____

    2. _____

    3. _____

Are any of these a problem with this person?

____ Yes ____ No

Have you communicated this to the employee?

____ Yes ____ No

What are the irrelevant behaviors? _____

_____

_____

What is the specific behavior in question with this employee?

_____

How frequently does this behavior occur? _____

What is the behavior you want to see? _____

_____

What current consequences are attached to this behavior?

    1. _____

    2. _____

When does the behavior take place? _____

Where does the behavior take place? _____

What factors do you control that are important to this employee? _____

_____

What factors are potentially unpleasant to this employee? _____

_____

_____

What strategies might be appropriate? _____

_____

Action Exercise
Manager/Employee Agreement Form

Date: _____

Employee: _____

Behavior in question: _____

New behavior target: _____

Time frame: _____

What will the employee try to do? _____

_____

How will both parties know when it has been achieved? _____

_____

_____

What will you as manager do—

- if the desired behavior is not reached? _____

  _____

- if the desired behavior is achieved? _____

  _____

- if only part of the goal is accomplished? _____

  _____

Review date: _____   [*Manager's signature*]

[*Employee's signature*]

Action Exercise
Exchange Agreement Form

Date: _____

Employee: _____

Performance behavior in question: _____

Frequency of behavior: _____

New target behavior: _____

Time frame: _____

How can the employee change? _____

_____

How will the parties know when this has happened? _____

_____

_____

What will you as manager do—

    • if the target is not reached? _____

    _____

    • if the target is reached? _____

    _____

    • if part of the goal is obtained? _____

    _____

Review date: _____ [*Manager's signature*]

                              [*Employee's signature*]

PART

Three

Turning On
Turned-Off Employees

Problems are in the "I" of the beholder.

ome horses are high-spirited, love to run free, and are often labeled "ornery" by their masters. When the horse rears and throws the jockey as the starting gate opens, who has a problem, the horse or the jockey? This section is about those difficult horses—the ones that regularly refuse to drink when asked, and sometimes won't even go near the water. The questions become "Why?" and "What can be done about it?"

Do you remember Br'er Rabbit? After years of frustration, Br'er Bear and Br'er Fox finally have Br'er Rabbit in their clutches. As they are debating what to do with him, Br'er Rabbit hits upon a marvelous strategy. He tells them to "boil me in oil," "skin me alive," but "just don't throw me in the brier patch!" Eventually, they get so frustrated with Br'er Rabbit that they say, that's it, no sympathy, and toss him into the brier patch. The brier patch is, of course, exactly where Br'er Rabbit wants to be. He has foiled them again! Do you have any Br'er Rabbits working for you? I hope so, because they are quite creative and enthusiastic, albeit mischievous, people. Smile, retain your balance, and manage them as creatively as they manage you!

Employees can be divided into three groups:

111

1. Average
2. Difficult
3. Abnormal

Average employees respond to the organizational reward and discipline system in predictable ways. These people comprise the bulk of any organization. The *difficult* employees behave in rational ways that are contrary to organizational norms but are surprisingly consistent and predictable. Difficult employees, though they constitute only a minority in the organization, can absorb an inordinate amount of their managers' time and energy. The third group of employees are those who exhibit *abnormal* behavior owing to severe personality disorders, sexual deviancy, or substance abuse. I am not a trained psychiatrist (probably you aren't either), so I suggest that while serious disorders be met with a caring approach, they should ultimately be turned over to trained professionals. Don't practice without a license!

Part Two should have given you the tools needed to deal effectively with average employees. Part Three deals with that middle group of infuriating, aggravating but rational, at times funny, sometimes lovable employees called "difficult people." Chapter 10 looks at how each of us is a problem to someone else. Chapter 11 examines the problem boss. Chapter 12 delineates the problem employee. And Chapter 13 explores problems that can arise in group meetings and activities.

Who is a problem person at work? Simply an employee who is either not doing what the manager wants or is not doing it the way the manager wants it done. Notice that anyone can be a potential problem employee. Also, realize who has the problem— the manager! The boss is the one who wants something to change. People can get turned off at work from a variety of causes. They can be turned off by the organization, by their job, or by you and me. Once they are turned off, as so many workers are, we need to understand them, decide what we want to have happen, and then develop strategies to accomplish that. I hope this section can help with your frustration regarding problem employees and ultimately reduce the number of tread marks they leave on your body from these "close encounters of the strange kind."

One helpful way to view your interactions with these "irregular people" is as short "dramas." In these dramas there is naturally a villain, a victim, and perhaps even a hero or heroine. Each character enters on cue, speaks his lines just as he did in the last performance, and exits dramatically. The same bad feelings set in.

Of course these people bug you, but possibly I can help you to get debugged. In dealing with difficult people, the first thing you have to decide is how much responsibility you have to each of your problem employees, to the organization you all work for, to yourself, and to your other employees. Don't expect big miracles. You're only human, and I don't have magic in my bag. But perhaps we can work a few minor "miracles."

Ultimately, if things don't work out with your problem people, you may have to install a progressive disciplinary program. A few difficult people are truly miserable, yet they can't bring themselves to quit their jobs. When you have honestly tried your best and the situation still hasn't changed, it may be time to help them fire themselves. Just remember what you learned in Chapter 5 about discipline without guilt, then act clearly, fairly, and consistently, and document it!

Prevention is naturally preferable to treating problem employees, and companies need to do a much better job of screening out potential problems. It seems often as if the immediate supervisor and human resources were taking a break when these problem personalities passed through. It is obvious that more direct contact is needed with those who knew the applicants for long periods of time, such as teachers, peers, and previous employers. Additionally, companies miss marvelous opportunities for shaping expectations and employee behavior during the indoctrination period. Most organizational indoctrinations are too short and shallow. The orientation period is the one chance a company has to teach new employees what it wants them to know about the organization, what the company is trying to do, and what it expects from them. Most companies, however, rush new recruits through orientation, then pay for it later as these new organizational members learn their expectations on the job from some malcontent.

Most important, you must try to maintain positive but realistic expectations as you learn and apply the material found in this section. If an employee is turned off, don't expect his behavior to change unless you can discover how to turn him back on. Sometimes that's easy. Often it's difficult. Occasionally it's impossible.

Matejka's Problem People Chart offers some hopefully humorous insight into the problem and should prepare you for what follows.

MATEJKA'S PROBLEM PEOPLE CHART

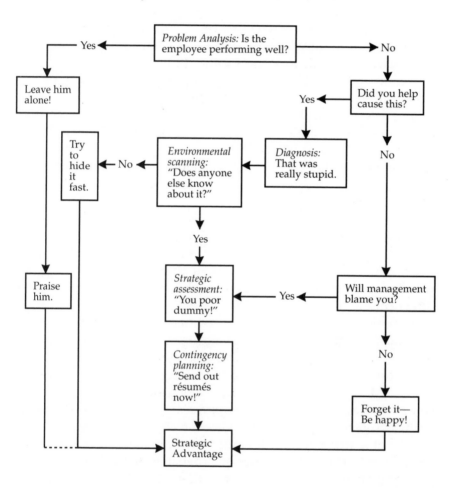

10

Managing the Problem Self

What counts is not how much you know about motivation, but how much motivation you show.

Any one employee is in some ways like all employees and in other ways like no employee. In that problem employees are defined simply as people who are not doing what the manager wants or not doing it in the way he wants, all employees at times can be considered problem people. I certainly create problems for my boss at times, and so do you. The key to the labeling of an employee as troublesome lies in the proportion of time spent in behavior that is undesirable.

Others judge us by our actions just as we judge them by what they do. Sometimes the actual reasons for our behavior are hidden from others. Therefore, behavioral conclusions are often based on incomplete data. Each of us overlooks certain aspects of our own behavior that others observe. Many managers act out the old "do as I say, not as I do" slogan. It's hardly fair to judge others by standards that we cannot or will not adhere to ourselves. Our behavioral responses to each other are based on and limited by our perceptions and experiences. In short, perception is distorted, yet that is the reality on which we base our behavior. Many times, understanding how your employees are perceiving you can be as tricky as trying to pick up Jell-O with a pitchfork!

Knowing Your Assets

Knowing your own personal strengths and weaknesses as a manager is important. But which set of personal assets and liabilities is more important?

- The strengths and weaknesses you actually have?
- The strengths and weaknesses you think you have?
- The strengths and weaknesses your boss thinks you have?
- The strengths and weaknesses your subordinates think you have?

As you can readily imagine, these four realities are different. Each party behaves according to his or her own perceptions. The potential for confusion and frustration is thus proportional to the amount of variance between any two perceptions. For example, suppose that you took a test on problem solving and that on a 1 to 5 scale (5 being excellent) you received a 4, you think you are a 5, your boss thinks you are a 3, and your subordinates perceive you to be a 2. Considering your high rating of yourself, it is likely that you believe you can solve just about any problem. Your boss and subordinates don't agree, however. As a result, your boss will probably not assign certain issues to you, and your subordinates may not come to you for help on tough decisions but instead will choose to decide for themselves. The potential for conflict in this scenario is great. You may feel hurt and perceive that your boss is playing favorites by not entrusting critical problems to you. You may feel angry with your subordinates for not coming to you with a difficult choice, especially if they have made a poor decision on their own. Or you may try to show them that they are wrong by taking on a difficult problem and perhaps leading with your weakness.

One way to discover these discrepancies is to take the direct route and find out what other people's perceptions actually are. To do this, you may want to hold separate exchange meetings, one with your subordinates and another with your boss, to share your perceptions of each other's strengths and weaknesses. Try to resolve the areas of difference that are revealed in this meeting by:

- *Proving*, using task opportunities or tests to show why your assessment is correct
- *Disproving*, demonstrating why their perceptions are incorrect
- *Improving*, through training or development
- *Approving*, agreeing with the new level of expectations

In general, the more *asset agreement* there is, the lower the potential for conflicting behavior is. This is especially true for technical skill levels but can also be significant for behavioral issues. On the downside, don't ask for a truthful evaluation of yourself unless you are ready to hear the truth as others perceive it and unless you are willing to change where necessary in response to the new information.

Exposing Blind Spots

If you think sunspots are hard to identify with the naked eye, try finding your own blind spots. Paradoxically, we all have a tremendous need for more self-awareness coupled with a personal reluctance to examine the level of our self-awareness. Considering the interest in the subject, it is not surprising that *Your Erroneous Zones*[1] was a runaway best-seller back in 1976. But whereas that book focused inward on our self-image, this chapter focuses outward on the perceptions of others, which cause their behavior. Blind spots are areas of our own behavior that we are not aware of but that others see. Much like horses equipped with blinders so that they will focus on the task ahead and not be diverted, human beings unwittingly place blinders on themselves that prevent them from seeing what is going on around them.

Blind spots are very easy to spot when others exhibit them. Take—

- the dog owner who isn't aware of the noise problem when her dog howls at midnight, or of the annoyance felt by her neighbors when the dog chooses their front yards for doing its business, or of the fear inspired by her pet after it has terrorized two joggers in the neighborhood;
- the otherwise normal, caring person who, when he gets behind the wheel of his car, becomes a menace, speeding down the road, cutting in front of other drivers, and turning without signaling;
- the absentee parents who, when presented with clear, convincing evidence of the antisocial behavior of their child, are appalled that anyone could think that Johnny was a problem; or

- the mechanic with four cars in various states of disrepair in his front yard who does not perceive the "sight pollution" experienced by everyone else in the area.

These examples suggest only a few of the infinite possibilities. We are all guilty of blind spots. The principle is beautifully illustrated by the situation you find on an athletic trail in a park when it is used by walkers, joggers, and bicycle riders. Each of the three groups develops its own blind spots. The joggers get irritated with the walkers moving three abreast and taking up virtually the entire width of the path. The walkers get angry with the joggers who expect them to move closer together to allow room for the joggers to pass. And both the walkers and the joggers are annoyed by the bikers who come up silently behind them and cut in, scaring and just missing them. From the biker's perspective, the walkers and joggers are weaving all over the place, making it difficult to decide where to aim the bike. Add to this scenario the fact that some groups are moving in the opposite direction while cars are also passing alongside in certain spots and you have the "havoc" of a pleasant half hour of exercise in the park. Perceiving the humor in this situation and laughing at everyone, including yourself, will remove some of the stress caused by blind spots.

Meanwhile, Back at the Office

Blind spots are as abundant in business organizations as anywhere else. Often they are caused by specialization. When people spend their entire careers in sales, production, accounting, human resources, finance, engineering, R&D, or market research, they develop a great deal of expertise in the functional area. But this expertise is often gained at the expense of having any vision with regard to the rest of the organization.

Suppose you decide to quit your job, move to North Carolina, and grow watermelons for a living. (Don't question the soundness of this move; just play along for a moment.) You buy some land and clear it, plow it, plant it, water it, fertilize it, and harvest it. Then you transport the crop and sell it. Now suppose that the whole business is costing you $1.50 per melon and you are trucking the melons to New York where you are selling them for $1.25 each. Sound farfetched? Not really. Many organizations operate at a loss. But what do you do? There is no dearth of people in your melon organization ready to give advice. For example:

- The salespeople think you must sell more, and want you to computerize your farm.
- The quality control people think you should grow better melons.
- The transportation specialists are convinced you need bigger trucks.
- The market research people question your target market.
- The finance people are looking for ways to better finance your debt.
- The R&D people are trying to come up with a square melon that will better utilize truck space.
- The human resources people think you need more training in group dynamics.
- The production people think the answer is new equipment.
- The field workers want higher wages.
- The environmentalists want you to stop using chemical fertilizers.
- OSHA thinks you ought to buy safer tractors.
- Your spouse thinks you should let the government pay you for *not* planting melons.
- The agricultural agent wants you to diversify with corn to replenish soil nutrients.
- Your accountant explains to you that you can't produce watermelons for $1.50 and sell them for $1.25.

This story may seem like an extreme exaggeration and foolish to boot. Unfortunately, it is all too common. Let me share another instance of the effects of specialization. I have had occasion to return two hams to two different retail grocers because I sensed they were spoiled. In the first instance, when I explained why I was returning the ham, I was subjected to a third-degree interrogation. When did I purchase the ham? Where did I place it? Did sunlight hit it? Did I open it prematurely? "Smells fine to me," said the manager! He spent ten minutes trying to convince me that I was the culprit who had wantonly abused a perfectly good ham. I have not been back to his store since. On the second occasion, the grocer—a different grocer—did not question my perception. He did not try to convince me that my senses were in error or that I had mistreated his ham. He merely apologized without question and told me to choose a larger ham and take it home without adjusting for the cost. I loyally purchased at this second store until I left the city a few years later, spending thousands of dollars over those few years.

The first grocer had an *accounting* mentality. Don't let some-one return a $30 ham if you can help it. He thinks he saved $30. Actually, he did. But it cost him thousands. The second grocer, who had a *business* mentality, understood that $30 was nothing compared to a satisfied, loyal customer. He also knew that I would tell this story to my friends and praise his approach, bringing in more word-of-mouth business. (The grocer was Ukrop's, which only operates in Virginia.)

Specialization is not the only culprit in creating blind spots. There are overall organizational blind spots produced by every-one in the organization being conditioned to think in a certain way. Growth may be pursued with no regard for profit. Innova-tion may be pushed with little concern for implementation. The culture can end up stifling needed discussion. Another potential blind spot is incrementalism. If we increased sales 5.1 percent last year and 5.3 percent this year, we're doing well. Meanwhile, the market is expanding at a rate of 22 percent and we're getting left in the dust. On a more mundane note, those endless, boring, unproductive meetings are usually the result of blind spots. It's ironic that when people look in the mirror, they see themselves reversed, not as others see them. Think about this, and make an effort to think of others' perceptions as a valuable, untapped resource.

Uncovering Your Hidden Biases

Biases are a little different from blind spots. Biases are prejudices (prejudgments) or preferences. They are subjective in nature and express an evaluation. They represent the "I may not know much about art but I know what I like" side of each of us. It is human to have preferences, but it is unfair and distasteful when we allow these predispositions to impinge on the freedoms and opportunities of other people. Prejudices can be costly to the organization in terms of lost potential efficiencies, sales, service, or profits. Some biases are overt, others covert. Sometimes we know we are biased and readily admit it. Other times we act subjectively and think we are being objective. Subjective preferences can affect the tasks we perform, the way jobs get done, or nonperformance-related (behavioral) issues.

Task Biases

Each of us prefers certain types of work. We may choose to spend our time on the big-picture stuff or on filling in the details. Some people love planning; others think it is a waste of time. Depending on your personality, you will gravitate toward one perspective or the other. Unfortunately, both perspectives are needed for a complete evaluation. Some managers do what they like and dump the other tasks on their subordinates. This may or may not be effective, depending on the skills and preferences of the subordinates. The potential for conflict exists when a manager prefers structure and her subordinates want ambiguity.

What exactly should we be trying to accomplish as managers? Choices must be made. Some things will be pursued, others neglected. While this is natural, a manager must fight the urge always to do what is familiar and comfortable. It is important to concentrate on the tasks that will benefit the largest part of the organization, not just yourself.

"How To" Biases

Most of the biases being manifested around performance are "how to" biases. The work is getting done. The tasks are being accomplished. But the manager wants the work done in a different way. Some managers prefer an autocratic style and want their subordinates to be autocratic. For others, being participative is preferable. The key question should be: How will the change affect performance? If the change will increase productivity, then why not use it? If the change will only make you feel better, don't bother. Employees have a tough time accepting "pet peeves" as legitimate and necessary. Using up your influence on these personal style issues will deplete your "influence account" and leave it bare at a time when you really need to change behavior.

Behavioral Biases

We all selectively screen incoming data. We screen out what we don't want to see, hear, or think about. We let through the stimuli we want. This selective screening has a biasing effect on what we consider and how strongly we consider it. Similarly, we selectively screen what we see in other people. This partial information is then blown out of proportion. One of the results of this personal screening is the damaging act of labeling people. Labels create unfair limits. If I, through selective screening of your behavior, label you a loser, then I will treat you like a loser. If I "like" what I selectively screen and label you a "winner," I will treat you like a winner. Make no mistake about it, these labels can become self-fulfilling prophecies. Subordinates often become what we treat them like. This process can be especially damaging when our biases lead us to favor one sex, race, culture, age, or ethnic group over others.

In addition to placing labels on people, managers are often prejudiced by the first or last behavioral event involving a subordinate. Once a winner, always a winner. Or you are only as good as your last task. These actions can assume far more importance than they should.

Some managers prefer to create ambiguity regarding exactly what they consider important in the performance of a subordinate. This ambiguity then allows the manager to develop whatever performance criteria he wants to use and to arrange the criteria according to whatever order or priorities are convenient, thus ensuring that his favorite employee will always win. This practice is more common than we would like to admit.

Finally, even the manner of dress of subordinates is an opportunity for biases to cloud the evaluation of people. There are instances and jobs where being well dressed is essential, but the actual style is usually a matter of personal taste, not task-imperative. A few managers even go so far as to detest particular colors, associating them with personality characteristics.

Blind-Spot-of-the-Month Award

I believe that humor is necessary for most managers to be able to detect, dissect, and deal with their blind spots and prejudices. If we can't smile at ourselves and others, there is little chance that we will succeed in dealing with these frailties. One way of using insight and levity is to formalize the use of this statement: "That's what people who _____ say!" For example, when an engineer is laying engineering biases on the group as the solution to all the organization's problems, you could gently, with a smile, announce, "That's what engineers say!" This can be truly effective if said in a nonthreatening manner. At least that's what authors say!

As a final suggestion for infusing humor, how about a Blind-Spot-of-the-Month Award, given to an individual, department, or division? Tack it up on the bulletin board (but only if you work in a large organization where some anonymity is possible). If people respond favorably and with good humor to this tactic, perhaps you could expand it and have an end-of-the-year Blind Spot of the Year Dinner Roast! If it doesn't work and people aren't taking the award with humor and gaining awareness, drop it. Some people take their blind spots much too seriously to learn from them. And besides, as I mentioned earlier, martyrdom is overrated.

Note

1. Wayne W. Dyer, *Your Erroneous Zones* (New York: Avon Books, 1976).

Action Exercise

Ask yourself and your subordinates the following questions:

1. What is it that you would like me to know about myself that I am not aware of?

   _____

   _____

2. What would I like you to know about me that you are not aware of?

   _____

   _____

3. What would I like to tell you about yourself?

   _____

   _____

Action Exercise

Choose a particularly difficult problem at work and ask your subordinates to come up with as many solutions as they can think of—

1. from their point of view: ————————————————

   ————————————————————————————————

2. from your point of view: ————————————————

   ————————————————————————————————

3. from another functional area's point of view: ——————————

   ————————————————————————————————

4. from the customers' point of view: ——————————

   ————————————————————————————————

*In which area did your people have the most trouble brainstorming?

————————————————————————————————

11

Managing the Baffling Boss

In a trail ride, the scenery changes for the lead horse and rider while everyone else is painfully aware that they are following a horse's behind!

Ahhhh, the baffling boss—that perverse purveyor of poor performance, that king of calamity, that prince of lost productivity, that sultan of slipping sales, that maharaja of malcontent, that lord of lost opportunities, that count of confusion! He couldn't tell there was Limburger cheese in the bag without opening it! He wouldn't know the difference between lightning and lightning bug! It's fitting that the baffling boss is Chapter 11—the financial equivalent of bankrupt and belly up!

OK! Now that we've got that out of our system, perhaps we can settle down and examine what is going on in this situation. I don't have any magic elixir, but I believe I can help you to see the situation more clearly. Some bosses exhibit what their subordinates perceive as "strange" behavior. These bosses are in a position of authority in our top-down organizations and therefore they are harder to influence than subordinates. But you can influence others, including your boss, to behave differently at times. Besides, have you noticed how one or two of your peers have become experts at getting what they want from the boss? It may seem strange to talk about managing your boss, but that is exactly what a manager tries to do when he decides that a change is advisable. When the boss is impossible to work for, the manager still has several options. The choices, however, are more limited than they are when you deal with subordinates. To give managers some useful guidance, and of course have some fun, this chapter will help you—

- evaluate your own power position;
- define the proverbial "baffling boss";
- explain why most baffling bosses behave as they do;
- illustrate some typical behavior patterns of baffling bosses;
- provide strategies that may help lead them to greener pastures; and
- suggest some "escape routes" in case nothing else works.

As adults, we have free will, make choices, and are responsible for our actions. It is important to run out of scapegoats. We can do anything we want; we just have to live with the consequences! Do something different—just think through the consequences. A good place to start is to ask yourself, "What is the worst thing that can happen if I constructively try to manage my boss?" Many times we exaggerate the potential consequences. On the other hand, if you continue to do what you have been doing, nothing will change. Take a good look at your boss and learn to see this baffling person as the caricature he or she is. Most baffling bosses are funny! Appreciating the comedic aspect of the baffling behavior will help you to maintain your own balance and give you a new perspective on the situation.

How Potent Is Your Power Position?

How much power do you have? Whether you are operating from a position of strength or a position of weakness will predetermine the advisability of some actions. In most organizations, your task expertise is the single largest determinant of your power. If you are the best at what you do, you can exert much more influence than if your performance is questionable. When you are the best, it is harder to replace you.

Beyond job skill, consider the way your particular organization would view your credibility vis-à-vis that of your boss. Some organizations see little difference between two adjoining levels of authority. Other companies exaggerate them. The acceptability of a subordinate questioning the actions of a superior is largely a function of the organizational culture regarding levels of authority.

Finally, consider the delicate question of the power of your personality. Two managers holding the same position exert varying degrees of influence depending on their personal attractiveness. For example, JFK and LBJ both held the position of president. LBJ was a master at manipulating the political system and therefore influenced Congress significantly, whereas JFK exerted more influence with the American people because of his charismatic personality. Are you disliked, liked, well liked, or very well liked by organizational members? Are influential people in your corner? How "well wired" are you?

The answers to these three questions should give you some indication of your power position and suggest what actions on your part might be acceptable and/or effective. You are responsible for objectively evaluating your own potential for influencing your boss. Miscalculating your power position could lead to adopting inappropriate strategies. Don't let a miscalculation of your strengths serve as a do-it-yourself termination kit!

Defining the Baffling Boss

"Let me tell you about my boss. If he ever said anything nice about my work his face would break!" We have all had similar thoughts about certain bosses. What is a baffling boss? When does an ordinary manager become a difficult boss? A baffling boss is merely any supervisor who is perceived by his or her subordinates as being difficult to comprehend (confusing), difficult to please (unrealistic), difficult to nail down (slippery), difficult to change (rigid), difficult to tolerate (crude), or difficult to respect (incompetent). Curiously, except for the inconsistent boss, baffling bosses tend to be so uniform in their behavior that they act very predictably.

The baffling boss is exasperating. This is partly because of the boss's unusual behavior and partly because of the desire of most subordinates to be accepted by the authority figure. These bosses leave their people exhausted, frustrated, and angry. Baffling bosses have styles that range from negative to argumentative to manipulative to incompetent to offensive. Subordinates view most of these behaviors as counterproductive, compulsive, or just plain "odd." Technically, the boss becomes a problem whenever he is perceived as a problem by his subordinates. Subordinates perceive the boss as difficult in the following situations:

- The boss isn't accomplishing the organizational goals. This boss is ineffective, incompetent, selfish, or just plain tired. The issue is lack of performance.
- The boss isn't doing what you want him to do. This represents a difference in priorities and goals.
- The boss isn't doing things the way you want them done. Behavioral style is the issue.
- The boss and you have a tough time communicating. The relationship is the issue.
- The boss is having difficulty learning his new role. The issue is experience.

It is important to determine whether the boss is a baffling person, handling a baffling job, creating a baffling relationship, or is baffling relative to the organizational culture. On the other hand, it is equally important to consider whether you are baffling to the boss and what causes this diversity. You should approach a clash of personality traits differently from the way you approach a question of organizational "fit."

Why Do Baffling Bosses Act Like That?

There are probably as many reasons for baffling behavior as there are individual baffling bosses. First, realize that the unusual behavior is being reinforced, either externally or internally. Baffling bosses are choosing, in their own psychological world, what will bring them more pleasure or less pain. Second, it is important to determine whether you are part of the problem. Do your peers perceive the boss as baffling? If they don't, perhaps you ought to look inside yourself for some answers. But if your peers concur with you, then there are some general possibilities that would apply to most difficult superiors.

- Some interpersonal conflicts are caused by a lack of behavioral understanding. The boss may have been a technician who is having a tough time trying to understand the important interpersonal behavioral nuances in handling people. This person can be helped to see the potential performance improvement that comes from paying attention to behavioral cues.

• Some bosses are living out the Peter Principle, having risen to their own level of incompetence. These people are frustrated because they would rather be back where they feel comfortable. Understand this frustration and help them where you can to build confidence and to progress.

• Some bosses are bitter about what has happened to them in the organization. They may have been passed over for promotion or had their ideas stolen. Be a constructive ally.

• Some bosses feel powerless because of a lack of involvement in organizational decision making. Understand their situation and try to help them build power so that your group can get what it needs in the way of resources.

• Some bosses are merely acting out of habit. They are unable to see when conditions have changed, warranting different behavior. Praise what works for you and be straight about what is hindering performance.

• Some bosses have huge blind spots about their behavior. Although this can be true of the autocratic manager who doesn't perceive the advantages of employee involvement, it usually refers to the boss who is exhibiting deviant behavior such as alcohol or drug abuse, sexual harassment, or just plain slovenly appearance. This person needs to be approached in a gentle, caring way by subordinates. He is still the boss until relieved of his position. Tread, but tread constructively.

Many times, the behavior of a baffling boss creates a conflict that ought to be resolved. What approach should you employ? Sometimes it's best to leave the situation as it is in order to buy time. When you are operating from a relatively weak position, brushing it aside is often prudent. If you have the power, forcing the issue may work. Bartering might be effective in cases where you both have something the other wants. You may even decide to "turn it over" to someone else. Finally, if a supraordinate goal (bigger than both of you) can be used as the focus, perhaps constructive collaboration can occur.

Typing Baffling Bosses

Baffling bosses come in many shapes and sizes, but they have a few similarities. First, there is abundant evidence that most employees agree that these supervisors are indeed baffling. Second, for the most part, these bosses behave in consistent patterns (except, of course, for the inconsistent boss). Employees know what they are going to do before they do it. Third, the motto of difficult bosses is usually "It's not my fault," which allows them to blame everyone else for whatever goes wrong. Fourth, dealing with difficult bosses drains an unusually high amount of strength and energy from those working under them. Fifth, sooner or later, the behavior gets blown out of proportion to reality, and mind-sets on both sides become rigid and not open to objective discussion. Sixth, it becomes easy and occasionally great fun for either party to push the other's "hot button," which is often worn on the lapel with great pride. Obviously they know your hot button or you wouldn't be so upset with them.

A baffling boss can be of any gender, race, color, or creed. No one group has a corner on the art of bafflement. In this section I attempt to "profile" some common types of irregular bosses and to provide some possible tactics for dealing with them. Here they are, the "Ten Most Unwanted"!

The Inconsistent Boss

If subordinates could ask for one trait in a boss, they would most likely choose consistency. After all, it's easier to deal with a consistent SOB than with a flip-flopping fish. Consistency allows employees to anticipate and plan. Inconsistency creates the worst case of management by mind reading. Guessing what this boss will do next is akin to taking your chances on the "Wheel of Misfortune"! Sometimes this type of person is just being "difficult," playing devil's advocate. Sometimes he only "seems" to be changing his mind because the employee misread the response last time. Often, the inconsistent boss is well meaning. That may sound strange, but very few people in this world change their minds just to be stubborn. Often what is really happening is that this person responds more strongly to recent information and is trying to be flexible. Unfortunately, too much flexibility can create Plastic Man. Try to find out the reason for the switch in direction. Say, in a straightforward, calm, nonthreatening way, "You appear to have changed your mind. Is that true? If so, what new information led you to make the switch?" Try to extract a specific answer. If the boss tries to dance around it, ask for a specific reason. Believe it or not, there often was one. Find it! Don't forget to tell the boss how helpful consistency is to your existence. Praise the behavior that you would like to see increased.

All the baffling types that follow are terribly consistent; ironically, their subordinates often wish they weren't. Deviations by these people would be breaths of fresh air.

The Indomitable Boss

Stand at attention, get those shoulders back, look straight ahead, and don't speak unless spoken to. The Supreme Commander has just come aboard! The "utter autocrat" is indeed a difficult superior and a formidable foe. This boss is totally independent in his thinking and judgments. He sees no point in seeking the opinion of others because no one else is as knowledgeable. It's his way or the highway! Delegation of anything important has never crossed his mind. The indomitable boss has a strong need to be decisive, correct, prescriptive, aggressive, and self-confident.

In dealing with the autocrat, remember these needs. This boss will respect expertise and strength, but don't embarrass him. Stand up for yourself, firmly. If you let the autocrat push you around at will, he will not respect you or your opinions. Don't react the way he expects you to; everyone else does that. This person has authority over you, and fear is natural, but try your best to be firm and constructive. Recognize his need to be correct, but help him to find the "right" answer. It may be beneficial to again ask yourself, "What's the worst thing that could happen?" Yes, I see what you mean. But remember, you are dissatisfied with the way things are.

The Incompetent Boss

A boss without the necessary task skills can be particularly hard to handle. Whether this boss is an old-timer whose knowledge has not kept pace with the changes in the field or simply someone who lacks the necessary managerial and/or technical expertise, the problem is to help him change. If the problem is a lack of ability, the best you can do is to take some of the responsibility on yourself and assist the boss in learning what he can. If the problem is outdated knowledge, there is a chance that you can turn him around. Remember, people who have not kept pace usually failed to do so because of a fear of the new technology or knowledge. Some didn't feel comfortable even trying. Take things one step at a time. Whether it's a new process, a modern management approach, or becoming computer-literate, teach them. If you can build some little successes, the boss may get turned on. I have witnessed some great turnarounds in business, government, and academia. It is a real joy to see someone who had virtually quit growing get turned on and adapt to the new demands. Education doesn't always work, but when it does, the reward is doubly pleasing.

The Indecent Boss

This character does not conform to accepted standards of propriety or good taste. The behavior of these bosses is improper and often offensive. Whether it's someone with bad breath, body odor, uncombed hair, or lunch on his beard or tie, someone who forces you to share his cigar smoke, or (in more serious cases) someone guilty of substance abuse or sexual harassment, these bosses violate societal norms. The indecent boss has a serious blind spot. (In the more extreme cases, what makes matters even worse is that the indecent boss expects his subordinates to make excuses or cover for him. Guilt pervades this setting. Deceit weaves its ugly web and turns work into a place no one wants to go.)

The best approach is to show serious, caring concern. A light touch may help the slob see himself as others see him. Humor is a useful tool when food stains cover his tie. But for progress to take place, humor must be followed by assertive requests to be more considerate with the cigar smoke. The more deviant forms of behavior, such as alcoholism and sexual harassment, must be treated seriously, caringly, firmly, and discreetly. It may be advisable at this point to discuss the problem with your company's human resources people. They are usually much better informed and better prepared to deal successfully with such individuals. You can even present the situation in a hypothetical way to get their advice before deciding on how to proceed. The indecent boss will have a tendency, even when aware, to deny much of the guilt. Depending on the advice from human resources, some facts may have to be gathered and documented. Strategically, don't put this boss down; just express your concern and a willingness to help in whatever way you can. The deviant boss needs professional help. Don't play amateur psychiatrist. Just be a friend if the circumstances permit you to be.

The Indispensable Boss

The indispensable boss has an ego problem. No one can do anything without her help! Looking over other people's shoulders is a vital preoccupation that shows distrust for the skills of her subordinates. This boss isn't a boss but a worker. The indispensable boss may have been a good technician who got promoted and now is unable to make the break from worker to manager. The indispensable boss frustrates people because she treats them like children who can't be trusted to perform on their own.

Managing this boss requires taking a two-pronged attack. On the one front, employees need to show Old Indispensable how this behavior is not only hurting performance but also hindering her own career. On the other front, subordinates must prove that they are fully capable of handling the tasks, and show how even mistakes are a learning experience that will bear fruit in the long run. Convincing this boss is not easy, however, because she has a fear of failure.

The Introspective Boss

The silent type can be infuriating as a boss. People who have never felt comfortable expressing themselves verbally create miscommunications and sometimes no communications between themselves and their subordinates. They deprive their subordinates of almost all feedback.

When dealing with this difficult boss, allow her a little time to reflect and communicate, but assertively ask for feedback. Help the introspective boss to understand that you are not like her and that the more information she shares, the easier it is for you to do your job.

The Incompatible Boss

When the boss's work style and your work style are at odds, the potential for conflict exists. The styles may be terse versus pensive, autocratic versus participative, practical versus theoretical, or friendly versus distant. It is unrealistic to expect the boss to change drastically. An effective working relationship with a boss accommodates these differences in work style.[1] For example, if the boss is easily distracted or bored during meetings and wants a minimum of details, develop brief, factual summaries of topics, and if a discussion is needed, explain why. Adjusting your style in response to your boss's preferences can reap dividends. If your boss is auditory, brief him personally. If he is visual, prepare a memo or a chart. If the boss has a high need for involvement, include him briefly and early in your own projects. Look at it this way: If you and your boss are opposites in some areas, together you can cover the needed bases. Meet him partway.

The Intolerable Boss

Many of the bosses already described are intolerable. The special case that should be singled out here is the sadistic boss who loves to inflict pain. He puts down, belittles, demeans, or humiliates at least one employee, and often steals ideas from all of his people.[2] It is helpful to know that such a person is insecure. Because he doesn't feel very good about himself, he tries to make others look bad in order to feel comparatively all right. Don't play! Getting into a battle of wits is suicide; he is an expert at sarcastic put-downs. Stand straight, talk straight, act straight. Compliment him when he passes up an opportunity to strike. Make him aware of those workers who really should not be subjected to his behavior. Ask him to be serious for a moment and to communicate his thoughts. Usually, a sincere, thoughtful question brings him back to a "thinking" rather than a "reactive" mode. If this boss steals your ideas, document them and publicly share the next idea before he has a chance to claim it for himself. Half a loaf is better than none.

The Irritable Boss

Anything sets this person off. Like Rambo, the irritable boss lurks, waiting for a screwup. If none occurs, this boss will create one. Nothing seems to please him. Just when you have busted your butt on a task, the irritable boss will find some reason to be displeased. Temper tantrums abound. Remain calm and ask for what you want. You can take the wind out of his sails by asking how you could improve on something before he has a chance to find fault.

The Indecisive Boss

Some bosses ride the range looking for outlaws. The indecisive boss rides the fence! There are two possible reasons why this boss can't decide. First, it may be the paralysis of analysis. Some bosses want more information before choosing. Of course, they can take this to the extreme and keep on not deciding until the time runs out. The second explanation is that this boss has a great fear of failure. Many people become paralyzed when faced with decisions. They feel very strongly both ways. You can help by providing whatever additional information is required to make the decision occur. This is a marvelous opportunity for you to sway the boss toward the correct decision, or at least the one that will assist you in accomplishing your goals.

One of the great myths perpetuated in organizations is that bosses actually know how to manage people. Most bosses have been trained in technical areas and have very little comprehension of how to manage subordinates. With this lack of education, much of what transpires is trial and error. But the myth gets perpetuated because the managers' insecurities won't let them tell the truth. Bosses often delude themselves about their own abilities in motivating and managing human resources, and subordinates, for their part, often insulate them from the truth. The myth lives on and it's not likely to die any time soon.

What Are the Options?

Because baffling bosses are so numerous, most of us have encountered one or two in the past, and it is quite likely that we will meet one or two again in the future. What can we do? There are several generic strategies available, some of which have been obliquely suggested in the last section.

1. *Do nothing.* The option of doing nothing is always present. Maybe you don't hurt enough yet. Maybe the boss will get hit by a truck, receive a transfer, or be promoted. In fact, in that good old American game of finding the boss a better job, you might be willing to write a great recommendation letter for the baffling boss just to get rid of the sucker. Tolerating the status quo is a better choice than doing something rash and counterproductive. Buying some time while you plan your strategies is a viable option. But doing nothing usually means continuing to do just what you have been doing—complaining, scheming, or slacking off. This seems appropriate only if you or the boss will be leaving soon.

2. *Escape.* There are plenty of bosses and companies out there; some of them are excellent. Sometimes it is very rational to think of getting out from under the baffling boss. Strategically, you might begin to talk to others inside and outside the company regarding the availability of positions and upcoming openings. I don't advocate running away from problems on a routine basis, but I have seen people who changed jobs go from night to day and increase their psychological well-being immensely. Life is too short to spend years in an intolerable setting. If you decide to stay on with the company, look for a particular boss you would like to work for and make that person casually aware of your desires. Don't give the impression of "running away"; you are, after all, "running toward" something better—with luck, much, much better.

3. *Manage the baffling boss.* Sometimes you may find yourself in a position where your options are limited, maintaining the status quo is intolerable, and escape isn't appropriate. In these circumstances, managing the boss is the only viable alternative. Managing a boss is of course more difficult than managing subordinates, but when managing the boss is necessary, there are several strategies you can use.

First, you must learn the boss's strengths and weaknesses and match these with your own. Many smart employees are dumb when it comes to understanding their own bosses. They either are too concerned with themselves or are trying too hard to impress the boss to take time to simply learn what the boss is like as a person. What does he need? What does he want? What are his organizational and personal goals? What could he use help with? What are his values? What bugs him? What energizes him? What does he fear? If you can answer these questions about your boss, you can manage him. You may decide to give him what he wants to get what you want. Or you may decide to meet him halfway. When you meet the boss's constructive needs, the boss will need to have you around. The more indispensable you are to the boss, the better he will treat you. The boss needs you and you need the boss. Give the boss some of what he needs and wants so long as it doesn't compromise your integrity. For example, suppose that your baffling boss likes to feel important whenever other VIPs are visiting the area. Would it hurt you to refer to him as "boss" or Mr. Smith if that enhanced his image?

Become a caring, constructive ally. Support the boss when he's right or even when you're not sure that he's wrong. Remember, if your goal is indeed a more effective relationship with your boss, then reinforcing what's helpful and right is not brownnosing. Both of you should benefit from this reciprocal relationship.

Don't hesitate to ask the boss questions. Stand up to intimidation. Walk tall, talk straight, but think about the boss, not just yourself. Your strategy may be dictated by how well the boss takes criticism, how well the boss listens, and how much the boss cares about the tasks and the people.

Of course, if you really have no interest in what the boss thinks, and have more fun complaining than contributing, then managing the boss to a better relationship isn't actually your goal, is it?

4. *Circumvent the baffling boss.* If you love the company and enjoy your job, then you may want to consider going to your boss's boss. This move is dangerous and can easily backfire, so use it only as a last resort. Organizations aren't necessarily "just" any more than life is. What you have to gauge are the organizational norms, the seriousness of your boss's behavior, the loyalties of the big boss, and your own needs and options. If you guess wrong and the boss and his boss hate employees who skip the chain of command, you could be punished in a variety of

ways: by performance ratings, loss of choice assignments, your boss's refusal to recommend you for advancement, or loss of salary increases. On the other hand, some big bosses want to hear what's going on below. If you do decide to talk with the big boss, at least approach it from a caring, not a resentful, standpoint. "How can I help?" is more palatable than gripes about "that SOB." Also, try to pick the right boss to go to, be totally prepared, and remember—there is strength in numbers; if others feel the same as you do, go as a group! If the behavior in question is immoral, unethical, or illegal, just make sure how high up knowledge of this behavior goes before you blow the whistle internally. If it goes high enough, your only recourse may be to document the activities and seek external help, such as by filing a lawsuit.

The Baffling Boss: That's a Wrap!

I have tried in this chapter to present a few descriptions of the most baffling types of bosses and to suggest some ways of dealing with them. (There are obviously many other types of bosses and strategies that I have not addressed.) The baffling boss presents an opportunity for you to be firm, sensible, and innovative. Consider the risks of acting versus the risks of not acting. Finally, why not compare your thoughts and reactions with those of your peers and friends. They may not see things as you do, which will cause you to rethink the situation. They may have some novel ideas. But since they don't feel what you feel, the final choice is yours. Make it wisely, after careful deliberation.

Notes

1. John J. Gabarro and John P. Kotter, "Managing Your Boss," in Leonard A. Schlesinger, Robert G. Eccles, and John J. Gabarro, eds., *Managing Behavior in Organizations* (New York: McGraw-Hill, 1983), pp. 210–20.
2. Mardy Grothe and Peter Wylie, *Problem Bosses* (New York: Fawcett Crest, 1987), p. 6.

Action Exercise

Understanding your boss is the key to managing him or her. Answer the questions below as best you can. For questions that you find difficult, observe and question your boss in those areas to gain further insights.

1. What does your baffling boss want to happen at work? _____

   _____

   • What can you do to help make it happen? _____

   _____

   • Would these actions violate your integrity? _____

2. What does your baffling boss need? _____

   _____

   • How could you help fulfill your baffling boss's needs? _____

   _____

   • Would this violate your integrity? _____

3. What does your baffling boss value most? _____

   _____

   • How could you meet your baffling boss halfway to achieve his/her values and yours? _____

   _____

   • Would these actions violate your integrity? _____

4. What are your baffling boss's pet peeves? _____

   _____

   • Could you exchange one of your boss's for one of yours? _____

   _____

   • Would this violate the integrity of either of you? _____

12

Managing Difficult Employees

When the manager asked his subordinate what the report he was working on was "about," the subordinate replied that it was "about fifteen pages"! The manager thought the subordinate was being "difficult."

ost employees are fairly hardworking, relatively dedicated, and respectful of authority. Getting the average employee to do what you want is usually so easy it isn't really challenging. All that is necessary is to be crystal clear about what you want, creatively connect it to the person you want to do it, give timely feedback, and reward good performance! When this sequence fails to produce the desired behavior, we often label the person who did not do what we wanted a "problem employee." The handling of those subordinates who refuse to "get on board" with our goals and needs is a major issue in the art of management. Difficult employees are a real challenge to your abilities as a manager.

Difficult employees can be grouped into three categories: major misbehavers, moderate misbehavers, and minor misbehavers.

Major misbehavers (like abnormal bosses) are those employees who *chronically misbehave* because they are *not in control* of their own behavior. As I mentioned in the introduction to Part Three, these extreme individuals need professional help and should be directed to the appropriate sources.

Managing Minor Misbehavers

Minor misbehavers are regular employees who on rare occasions do something you wish they hadn't. These people are normal, law-abiding employees who occasionally and inadvertently get into a little trouble. When minor misbehavers don't do what you want, it is usually because—

- you aren't clear in general about what behavior you want,
- you haven't made what you want clear to the "doer" in particular,
- the consequences of compliance and noncompliance have not been made clear,
- the consequences are vividly clear but unbelievable (in other words, there is big talk but no action),
- the consequences seem inconsequential,
- the employee is not currently capable of performing the task as required,
- there are work obstacles beyond the employee's control, or
- the employee is experiencing temporary stress or frustration due to circumstances beyond his control.

To get minor misbehavers back on track, you have merely to communicate openly with them and to fix whatever is askew. The minor misbehaver is not malicious or chronic.

Managing Moderate Misbehavers

What I will tackle in this chapter is an explanation of the second group, moderate misbehavers. This middle group consists of normal employees who *chronically misbehave* (in the eyes of the manager) while *fully in control* of their thoughts and emotions. Moderate misbehavers are relatively normal people acting in what the manager perceives as undesirable ways. These subordinates represent the bulk of a manager's recurring, prime-time problem people. Are these problem employees born or made? The answer is, of course, yes! Some disruptive employees are genetically and/ or socially scripted for "being difficult" early in life. The manager who is unlucky enough to have these folks in her charge because the "people sorters" in human resources were asleep at the switch has her hands full! It is appropriate to shout, "Why me, Lord?" Although these "different" employees are in the minority, they can seem like the majority because of the disproportionate amount of time the manager ends up spending on them. If you have even one hard-core misbehaver in your group, life can become a polluted beach.

Why Do Employees Misbehave?

Normally, employees should be able to achieve personal goals while constructively working toward organizational goals. If the organizational systems (communication, measurement, and rewards) are set up logically, there's no problem. But when it's impossible to accomplish what they want through organizational channels, some employees will revert to undesirable work behavior to achieve more singularly selfish targets. Understanding why they are misbehaving is the key to knowing what to do to change their behavior. Most misbehavers can be grouped into categories according to what they are receiving from their work misconduct.

Recognition

This "game" is a grown-up version of "Look, Mom, no hands." People who play it want an inordinate amount of recognition. Looking for adult approval, they may throw temper tantrums, pout, whine, whimper, cry, or shirk responsibility by asking questions neverendingly. Over time, *attention addicts* can infuriate busy managers.

Once you realize that attention is what these problem people are seeking, the proper response is obvious. Communicate firmly, but supportively, exactly what you want and expect from the attention addict. People who want attention are usually insecure about themselves or the task. They will need reassurance that attention will come after they do what is asked, and that while learning, mistakes may occur. If a subordinate refuses to exercise responsibility and make a decision, strongly inform him that the issue is "deciding." Explain that you want a decision and that you will not interact with him until he has made it. Also, remember to reassure him that it is OK to be wrong, that you will talk with him about the quality of the decision later, but until he makes a decision, you will have no personal transaction with him. Attention addicts who are indecisive have not had any practice in deciding and may be fearful at first. Lend your support *after* they choose.

Domination

The ability to dominate or influence is what drives *power players*. Work becomes a constant battle for control. Games of one-upmanship, where the issue is "Mine is bigger than yours!" or "Who's more important?" are common. Verbal jousting, refusal to obey commands, subtle sabotage, and converting colleagues into allies are part of the power player's package. The top drawer is stuffed with "I told you so" memos, ready for distribution. Publicly embarrassing the boss is the ultimate victory for dominators.

If a confrontation is going to occur, it may as well occur early. But *you* should choose the time and the place (in private). Once you have constructively and factually asserted your position, the power player may even become a valuable ally, living off and enhancing your power. After the confrontation, be calm, fair, and accepting of the employee's needs for influence and saving face. If the fire is still simmering, postpone any discussion until both of you have had time to reexamine the issues reasonably and objectively.

Security

Some employees misbehave to disguise their own fears, frailties, and failures. Their personal defects can be real or imagined. The employee could need training or education to successfully tackle the task. But he might also be just a very capable person with an inferiority complex. Or he could be striving for unattainable perfection. In other words, the block can be lack of ability, lack of training, unrealistic expectations, or an unrealistic personal appraisal.

Some *disguise devotees* have a terrible self-image and refuse even to try. This fear of trying causes them to belittle the task. For example, suppose that a company decided to switch from manual to computer inventory control. The employees who have never used computers and are petrified by them would use up much energy trying to stop this change, or slow it down, or make it fail. They aren't bad employees, just scared. Most of them could make the adjustment with help, training, and emotional support. But change itself has many enemies. The change may cause some defects to surface. Think about someone who cannot read well but has been able to hide this fact from others. The new system will find her out. She will lose power and influence and be embarrassed. What would you do if you were in her shoes? Even the perfectionist could be upset by this shift in processes. In the short run, there will be more errors.

The manager must inform, educate, and lend emotional support to the disguise devotee. Most people can successfully make the switch, but to reduce the resistance they have, the manager must show them how they will personally benefit and how they can accomplish the shift. Establish very reasonable expectations for the employee and build the employee's confidence and expectations. These processes take time, energy, care, and support. Once the task has been mastered, the practice of "being there to help at any time" is unrealistic and paints a picture of dependency. Once the task is learned, the best strategy is neither to abandon nor to smother the employee.

Retribution

Employees who feel misused, deceived, baited, or badgered can become angry and strike back at the source of the irritation or at some third party. *Avenging aficionados* display tight jaws and tight fists. Trying to defuse these revengeful employees can be dangerous, but the manager must ensure adherence to the proper standards of work behavior.

There is little sense in telling yourself that this employee should not be or is not angry. The avenger is mad! The best course is to talk with him about—

- the perceived source of the problem;
- how the problem affects performance;
- how the problem prevents goal achievement;
- how the problem affects colleagues; and
- how the problem affects you.

Don't sugarcoat the message, but steer clear of any kind of personal attack. Urge the employee to develop some plan to reduce the stress felt and to diminish the anger. If the employee is mistaken, help clear that up. If all else fails, suggest counseling. The bottom line here is that you may have to toss in the towel on a hard-core avenger. Retaining an employee who is openly disrespectful of you and your authority is often a regrettable decision.

Challenge

Many creative people get bored on their jobs. When imaginative employees are prevented from expressing their innovativeness in their work, they strive to find some other way of using their ingenuity. *Inventive instigators* are merely compensating for lost, desired opportunities, but they can be talented pains in the neck! Occasionally, the creative employee's greatest delight is to engage the manager in a battle of wits. It's just a game that allows the talented employee a bit of mental exercise. But it can drive the manager to his wit's end.

It's usually a mistake not to confront the inventive instigator when the undesirable behavior first starts. Recognize this employee's need for challenges and channel that ingenuity toward organizational goals. Don't ignore it. It's more productive to discuss the clever aspects of the behavior and together brainstorm ways that this energy can be applied constructively toward task completion. Finding new ways to "enrich" the job can benefit the inventive employee, the manager, and the organization.

Comfort

When a good performer becomes a poor performer, the culprit is usually change. The change could have occurred on the job or off the job. Whenever tasks and competencies shift at work, there is a natural resistance. Most people are familiar and comfortable with the status quo. Alterations cause insecurities to surface. In any change, there are winners and losers, but most employees perceive a potential loss. On the other hand, even your best employees can become difficult subordinates when a personal crisis hits. When it's a family illness, irreconcilable differences with a spouse, the death of a child, or mounting financial burdens, the stress created can result in alcoholism, withdrawal, physical illness, or just plain irritability. Any time a good performer becomes a poor performer, the manager should look for the change that caused the behavior to shift.

If the change is off the job, use a caring, helpful approach, but ultimately professional help should be suggested. When the change is job-related, realize that the employee has lost something, or at least perceives a loss. Find out what the loss entails and help him to gain it back in other ways or see that the loss is not real.

Typing Difficult Employees

Now that we understand the basis for most undesirable behavior, that is, the need for—

- recognition,
- power,
- security,
- retribution,
- challenge, and
- comfort.

let me sketch some of the more common and cantankerous misbehavers and use their motivation to suggest strategies the manager can employ. These "types" are naturally not meant as complete or exact descriptions of specific "difficult" employees. Nor do these sketches exhaust the behavioral possibilities. The types can be male or female.

The Bully

Most departments seem to have at least one Bully, Bulldozer, or Armored Tank. If he had a name, it would be Billy Club. If she had a name it would be Barb Wire. The Bully is a loud, sarcastic, argumentative, intimidating individual. His battle cry is "Ladies and gentlemen, start your engines!" Her motto is "Reshape the landscape!" This employee runs right over anyone who gets in his way, including the boss if permitted. Reverse does not seem to be a viable gear, and he is too impatient to use neutral very often. The Bully refers to people as "idiots," "dummies," and "wimps." He can be nasty, curt, rude, abrasive, and just plain arrogant. The Bully sees his victims as weak and inferior. He slowly, methodically tramples everyone with continual, unending criticism and barbs. The Bully strives to excel, to win, and, most important, to be always right. He is overwhelming in interpersonal exchanges, garnering great power ceded to him by his willing and unwilling victims. This Bulldozer is bright but not popular. His peers suffer from withdrawal, anger, or submission. The Bully hates weakness, especially as exhibited by tearful losers.

The Bully has a strong need for power. Winning the interpersonal exchange, pushing his views on others, and being right are the keys to satisfaction. These difficult employees perceive the world in clear, concise terms. Tasks are straightforward, to be performed quickly. Impatience is a virtue. Confidence is never (on the surface) lacking. What *is* lacking is caring, support, and trust. What the Bully fears is discovering his own inadequacies and losing a battle or the war.

The Bully has a serious blind spot. He cannot accurately perceive his true impact on others and the tasks at hand. He charges into other people all the time, unable to differentiate the times when attack is appropriate from the situations where caring is needed. He often takes a difference of opinion as rejection.

Here are the best strategies for dealing with the Bully:

1. Stand up straight! (Refuse to be run over.)
2. Stay cool! (Don't fight or flee.)
3. Allow the Bully some time to tire out.
4. Maintain eye contact.
5. Get him to sit down. (If he stands, you stand.)
6. Voice your differences firmly.
7. Confront as needed.
8. Give the Bully the task of problem solving.
9. Afterwards, be friendly!

Don't expect the Bully to be able to see his own defects; remember, inability to do this is his particular blind spot. The Bully often has a lot to offer, but his manager must find ways to tone him down and tone the others up. After a controlled, objective, firm confrontation, don't be surprised if the Bully acts friendly. Be friends. This is akin to two brothers punching each other till a winner emerges, then putting their arms around each other and going out for a beer. When it's over, it's over. The Bully respects strength. Many times friendship with the victor is natural.

The Faultfinder

This employee hones in on the negative side of every issue like a heat-seeking missile. She is against everything. Nothing's gonna work. No use trying. Just forget about it! Also known as the grouch, the complainer, the whiner, or the crab, the Faultfinder chooses always to perceive the downside and blames others for the possibilities. While the Faultfinder does not inspire the hostility and fear the Bully does, she can be boring, irritating, and just plain tiring. Utilizing the power of negative energy, the Faultfinder wants to remake the world to her own specifications.

Like most problem employees, faultfinders can't see themselves as others see them. They think they are merely trying to help, not whining. Faultfinders' actions originate in a "powerless" view of the world. Control is perceived as beyond their grasp and therefore preordained. They are appalled that things are the way they are and not the way they "should be." Grousing about issues makes them innocent—they tried to warn us!

What does the Faultfinder receive that maintains this behavior? Mostly, her need is for attention, with perhaps some minor revenge thrown in. Faultfinders want everyone's recognition and want the manager especially to make things the way they "should be." Faultfinders do often point out real issues and legitimate concerns, but they frequently lack the objectivity, discipline, and strength to solve problems. What the Faultfinder really fears is taking initiative and risks. She doesn't really feel good about herself, but criticizing others allows her to feel superior to her intended victims.

What can a manager do for these people? First, really listen to what they are telling you. You may gain some general insights into organizational problems and some specific information regarding the person. Stick to one issue; don't let them ramble. Interrupt them when needed to ensure that they stay on the question or clarify. Don't allow faultfinders to use inappropriate generalizations; pin them down for times, dates, names. Acknowledge that you understand their point, but be clear if and when you do not agree. Summarize, state the facts as you know them, and assign the task of finding a solution to them. Problem solve with them to start the ball rolling. For example, when does it happen? Does it always happen? What are the exceptions? Who is involved? How can you tell if it's getting better or worse? Ask the Faultfinder what she wants. Tell her what you want. Ask her what is new or different. To end the interaction, state what you believe will happen—loudly, firmly, realistically, but optimistically.

The Nice Person

It's tough to manage someone who is agreeable, sweet, gentle, lovable, understanding—and unproductive. Whether it's a client or a subordinate, these people can drive a manager up the wall. The Nice Person is always smiling and tells great stories and jokes. But the problem with the overly nice person is that he doesn't communicate honestly. He tells you what he thinks you want to hear (management by mind reading), but won't share any unpleasant truths. Consequently, the manager doesn't get the feedback he needs. There is a difference between having a positive attitude most of the time and ignoring obvious negatives.

The Nice Person hates conflict. His approach to disagreement is to prevent it, avoid it, or smooth it over if it surfaces. The Nice Person needs an unruffled atmosphere and a pleasant relationship with the boss. When someone who grew up in a household where conflict was avoided (the Nice Person) interacts with a person who grew up fighting eight brothers and sisters for the last dinner roll (the Bully), one leans way back and the other leans way in.

To handle and help the Nice Person, question him frequently. Be specific: "What makes this such a good plan?" Refuse to accept impossible-to-carry-out promises. Ask for actions, not words: "Can I expect that big order on Thursday?" Stress the need for truthful criticism. In some ways, the Nice Person is the opposite of the Faultfinder. But hearing pleasant information constantly is as dysfunctional for the manager as being exposed only to negative data. Neither behavior is very helpful to attaining organizational goals. Try to help the overly Nice Person to see that some conflict is necessary. Without conflict, we become complacent. Realize, though, that the overly Nice Person will err on the side of not confronting an existing problem. If you are "blessed" with both a Faultfinder and a Nice Person as subordinates, the truth will lie somewhere in between their responses. Try to make honesty and conflict nonthreatening to the Nice Person.

The Know-It-All

Didn't you just hate it in grade school when some kid seemed always to have the answers? No matter what the subject, the expert has an answer. Often the Know-It-All *is* right, which is truly infuriating. The Know-It-All is very impatient and thinks that her own individual intelligence and wit are the only standards for judging other people's performance.

The Know-It-All has a need for power, looks down on others, but actually may fear displeasing authority figures. The worst fear is not living up to her own standards of performance. Being right is more important than being considerate. The problem is that in acting this way, the expert causes such resentment that total productivity may fall.

When confronting the Know-It-All:

1. Don't argue.
2. Do your homework.
3. Give feedback.
4. Ask for additional possibilities.
5. Suggest your own alternatives.
6. Challenge her to problem solve.

Don't fight with her, but rather explore possibilities. Avoid trying to be the counterexpert. Question, listen, acknowledge, and explore.

The Postponer

The Postponer is an agreeable sort of person who means well. He does not postpone out of malice. Yet the Postponer can frustrate the accomplishment of your goals because he refuses to make a decision. The Postponer's game is to stay very general and to avoid having to decide on specifics. Somewhere in life, this person was reinforced for not deciding or punished severely for making a poor decision. Postponing allows him to avoid distress. A secondary need may be to avoid hurting the feelings of other employees.

Postponers obviously fear making mistakes. Not deciding allows them to cover up their perceived inadequacies (insecurities) and reduces the chance of failure. The blind spot for the Postponer is not perceiving his own unwillingness to take a risk. He continues to explore, gather more data, search for alternatives, forever—like the Ph.D. candidate who would rather do anything than actually begin writing his dissertation. This avoidance can become debilitating.

The solution is to try to find the reason for the Postponer's blockage and then help him to reorient his priorities and measures of success. In dealing with the Postponer:

1. Listen carefully to hear the reasons behind the words.
2. Be firm about your wants.
3. Be reassuring about his attempts.
4. Allow mistakes (make deciding the issue).
5. Insist on specifics and rankings of alternatives.
6. Negotiate precise time frames for a decision.
7. Avoid tempting put-downs.
8. Give support after a decision.
9. Help analyze the merits of the choice.
10. Explain how the behavior helps you.

The Postponer needs to be caringly held responsible for choosing. At first, the quality of the decision is not important. Deciding is what you want. If you create an atmosphere in which it's OK to make an inappropriate choice while learning, you reduce the Postponer's fears. What you want to establish is the "habit" of deciding. Next, work with him on the quality of the choice. Remove your attention until a choice is made.

When All Else Fails

In short, in dealing with problem or difficult employees, the real key is to discover what they are getting in return for their present behavior. Once you know what needs are being met by the undesirable behavior, a new way to satisfy those needs becomes the answer. Stop reinforcing the bad behavior. Instead, create a situation where it is possible for more positive behavior to occur.

But if you can't pull it off, if the behavior is just too bizarre and intractable, if the wounds are too deep, or if (for the sake of your own sanity) you need to end the situation, then dismissing the misbehaver becomes the only alternative. Before doing so, make sure that you have not only documented the behavior but that you have also warned the individual that a continuation of this specific behavior will result in dismissal.

As for the mechanics of firing someone, check with your professional human resources staff and consider the following tips:

1. If your human resources department agrees, it is often best to dismiss the misbehaver yourself; don't farm out the task. But be careful to follow human resources guidelines on "how."
2. Dismiss the employee in your office, where you are behind the desk and in control.
3. Ask the person to sit down.
4. Don't draw out the procedure. Dismiss the employee in a fairly quick manner. By this time, there's no sense arguing. The two of you probably have nothing else to say to each other.
5. If possible, dismiss the person on a Friday afternoon so you won't spend your weekend worrying about the confrontation.
6. Ask the person to clean out his office. It's not a good idea to let dismissed employees use their offices while looking for another job.

Firing people, when you have the authority to do that, is never pleasant. But sometimes they have ruined weeks, months, and even years of your life, and enough is enough! If you've been *straight* and *clear*, then they have really fired themselves.

Action Exercise

Think about your most difficult employee and find the specific answers
to these questions.

1. What is the specific behavior you want to change? _____

_____

2. What behavior is the employee currently exhibiting (be specific)?

_____

_____

3. What needs is the employee satisfying by his current behavior?

_____

4. How can you fulfill these needs in a positive way so that they
   will serve to reinforce the appropriate behavior? _____

_____

5. What must you stop doing? _____

_____

6. How can you firmly, clearly, and supportively communicate
   this? _____

_____

13

Leading and Managing Difficult Groups

Power corrupts. At least that's what people without power say.

re two heads better than one? Are sixty heads better than two? Is a giraffe really a horse designed by a group that wasn't afraid to stick its neck out? Most people have a built-in preference either for working alone or for working in groups. Our individualistic society seems to have a natural bias against group decision making. Yet the dynamic, changing social and technological environments of the 1990s will increasingly demand the use of groups to decide issues. When survival is at stake, pooling our knowledge makes great sense. The emerging truth seems to be that groups are becoming more important as decision-making tools in our organizations because of:

- The rate of change in the world
- The proliferation of knowledge
- The need for coordinated, integrated decisions
- A "pass the buck" mentality

Leading a group effectively can be a tough task even when the group is cohesive. Leading a group in which conflict exists can be truly "difficult," which is why I have included it in this section.

Some Group Characteristics

How do you know when you have a group? This may seem like begging the question. It is not. A group is usually thought to be two or more people who communicate, interact, and pursue a common goal. Even more important, a group must perceive itself to be a group. All the members must recognize all the other members as legitimate members of the group. This psychological identity is critical to the effective functioning of the group. In this perspective, the group exists only when it thinks it does.

There are many different types of groups. Groups can be—

- small, medium, or large;
- formal or informal;
- temporary or permanent;
- task-oriented or social;
- developing or mature;
- meeting frequently or infrequently;
- static or changing;
- homogeneous or diverse;
- independent, interdependent, or counterdependent;
- self-perpetuating or appointed.

Considering the possible combinations and permutations, two things become apparent: (1) Leading a group effectively takes great thought and skill, and (2) the adage that "a group is a group" shows a lack of ability to properly differentiate.

Some groups perform much better than others. The factors that determine the effectiveness of a decision-making group are—

- the personalities of the members;
- the leadership exerted by the manager;
- the roles assigned to members;
- the norms that emerge;
- the relative attractiveness of group membership;
- the dominance of one or two individuals;
- the insulation of the group from outside ideas and consid- erations; and
- the process used by the manager.

As you can see, there are many potential pitfalls to avoid before arriving at a useful and accurate group decision.

Management vs. Leadership

Should you manage or lead a group? The answer is yes. Do both! I wrestled very hard with whether it was more appropriate to entitle this chapter "leading" or "managing" difficult groups and decided that both words were necessary. Most of the current controversy regarding management versus leadership is much ado about nothing much! Peter Drucker's popular statement that "managers do things right while leaders do the right things!"[1] is an attempt to bring vision, intuition, and morality into the equation. But it creates a somewhat artificial distinction.

Management and leadership are slightly different, mostly related, and certainly needed in combination. A *leader* is someone who takes initiative, and a *manager* is someone who guides. Hardly a huge difference. In fact, it would seem that both capacities are necessary if one is to be an effective person. Initiating action without the skill to guide the accomplishment is foolhardy. Likewise, guiding activities without the vision to initiate can sometimes be counterproductive. Certainly leaders need vision to initiate action. We need more leaders. A leader can, however, be a fighter or a healer, a builder or a destroyer. And a manager who "guides" expertly would seem to be initiating action toward a vision. To some people, leadership sounds more exciting. But remember, the true difference lies in the proven "vision" of effective leaders. Vision is a critical concept, as I will show in the following chapters.

Despite the overlapping of the two concepts, I can make three statements about leadership and management with relative certainty:

1. We know much more about management than we do about leadership, even after studying it for decades.
2. Much of leadership is built on charisma, which cannot be taught.
3. We need more good leaders.

For the remainder of this chapter, I will deal mainly with the important elements of groups that need to be managed.

Managing the Group Process

Some things are inevitable with groups. Groups go through developmental stages, typically forming, storming, norming, and performing.[2] The group is assembled, either formally or informally. Next, the participants go through a shakedown in which differences of opinion emerge and create conflict. Then the group works its way through this conflict and establishes its own pattern of coping and acceptable behaviors. Finally, the group uses these parameters to perform the tasks at hand.

Some intragroup conflict is bound to occur. Conflict can be useful or destructive, depending on the amount of it and on how it is handled by the manager. Different personalities, values, ways of doing things, and personal goals, together with competition for resources, can all cause friction. However, these diversities are needed if a thorough and open analysis is to take place. As manager, your job is to control the conflict in one of six ways, by doing the following:

1. Avoid conflict through consideration.
2. Discourage conflict through cooperation.
3. Encourage conflict through competition.
4. Minimize conflict through conciliation.
5. Resolve conflict through compromise.
6. Resolve conflict through confrontation.

All these strategies can be useful, depending on the group participants, the type of conflict, and the desired end result.

A different way of viewing the prodigious task of effectively managing the difficult group is to carefully consider two critical variables: power and participation.

Managing Power in the Group Setting

Power can be defined as the ability to affect the behavior of others. When you influence people, you get them to do something they would not have done without your intervention. Influence is akin to power. To be influential, the manager must have something that is important to his followers and something that they cannot easily get outside the relationship. The reciprocal is being powerful because you are not influenced by others. In a group setting, influence must be understood from three perspectives:

1. The influence that the leader/manager exerts
2. The influence of individual members in the group process
3. The influence that exists in the interactive group processes

Power is like air; it's everywhere. Power can be grabbed, expanded, built, sculpted, given, taken, assumed, inherited, won, lost, used, abused, feared, respected, or ignored. Power can be built through many avenues, such as:

• *Position.* The group leader has the formal authority and therefore is the legitimate initiator of action. The *power of the position* is the initial building block for the manager. The more clearly this position is defined, the less likely it is that conflict will arise. The more autonomy and authority that the superior gives to the group leader, the more solid the members' perception will be that the leader has the formal ability to influence others.

• *Proficiency.* Perhaps the single most important determinant of the amount of influence a manager has with the group is the manager's expertise. *Task expertise* will make people gravitate toward the manager automatically. If the manager knows more about the task than anyone else, and can solve problems that others cannot, the ability to influence is greatly enhanced. The group leader's task, however, is not to do everything for the group but to manage/lead the group. This means teaching others to become task experts too. This paradox is at the heart of ineffective management. Teaching others what we know increases the effectiveness of the department, but it also raises the fear of diminishing the manager's knowledge power.

• *Praise and Punishment.* A manager can build influence by utilizing the information presented in Chapters 5 through 9 of this book. Clear consequences administered in a consistent manner build a sense of security and trust in subordinates. Although the manager has certain legitimate avenues for applying rewards and punishments built into the position, the application of consequences in an informed, skillful manner enhances the ability to influence. The *power of clarity* provides an enormous advantage, and this is reflected in an increased ability to influence the group.

• *Preferences.* Another building block for influence within the decision-making group is the relative congruity of values among the manager, the group, and the organization. The *power of value congruence* is often overlooked. It is OK for the manager to differ on any given perspective. However, when there are too many points of departure between what the organization stands for, what the manager believes, and what the group holds dear, the manager's effectiveness is diminished. Diversity of opinion is natural, but too much disparity cannot be tolerated. The closer the manager's values are to the values of the group, the easier it is to gain influence, which can then be used to move the group smoothly toward the goal.

• *Personality.* As previously stated, the *power of personality* is important. I'm not saying that a manager has to be a dynamo, but it's easy to see what a difference it makes when an appealing personality is combined with other power bases, especially expertise. Some parts of personality are predetermined, but many aspects of how you're perceived as a manager are changeable. Work on your ability to show interest, enthusiasm, and passion. If the group leader isn't enthusiastic, why should the group members get excited?

• *Persuasion.* The skill involved in changing behavior to what seems to be only natural or right is a powerful ability. To exercise this skill, the manager must be able to get the attention of the group, provide understanding, and use argumentation and presentation skills to gain acceptance. The manager must learn how to "fit" the requests to the listeners' view of reality—packaging them in the listeners' language and terms, and using a hard or soft, rational or emotional approach depending on the composition of the group. Enthusiasm is the basic ingredient of effective persuasion. Whenever the task performance of a group leader is difficult to measure, personality and persuasion become the differentiating tools.

• *Politics.* A manager can gain power by knowing the distribution of power in the organization and by gaining proximity to and association with its influential people. Being a surrogate for the most powerful person in the company gives influence. Political activity is simply a matter of how competing preferences get resolved. You can utilize this process to overcome resistance or merely to enhance your position. Building your own personal power is necessary to your being able to effectively influence the group. It is also essential to influencing others in order to procure the resources that your group must have to perform well.

Balancing Group Participation

Sometimes circumstances dictate that the manager just tell the group what to do. Sometimes the manager must persuade members. Sometimes the manager is obliged to discuss options with them. Sometimes the manager has to let the group do it. As the variables in the situation change, so should the approach. But sooner or later, the manager will need to teach the group to conduct its business in an effective, efficient, involved manner.

Building a team takes effort and knowledge. The relative influence of each member of the group should be examined. The normative process that the group develops should be molded by the manager. Group members bring different levels of status, seniority, experience, responsibility, and expertise to the table. These built-in inequities can seriously impair input and commitment by suppressing individual members or minority opinions. Study your group to discover the following:

- Who speaks the most?
- Who commands the group's attention?
- Who is relatively silent?
- Who is ignored by the group?
- Who competes?
- Who cooperates?
- Who questions?
- Who summarizes?
- Who is negative?
- Who is speaking more or less than in the past?

For everyone to feel that they are part of the group, cliques should be discouraged. The group will be more effective, more creative, more influential, and more involved if input is shared.

An imbalance among members' opinions and "airtime" must be managed by the leader. Cohesion depends on the manager's ability to notice and expertly deal with differences in influence. Some possible strategies are as follows:

1. *Clarify what someone is saying to elicit agreement/disagreement and further discussion.* Example: "Fred, let's see if I understood your idea correctly." This will focus attention on Fred's thought and invite more explanation.

2. *Spread the discussion more evenly to gain unexpressed ideas.* Example: "Jane, what is your approach?" or "Tim, what does packaging think?"

3. *Deflect someone who tends to monopolize the conversation.* Example: "Thanks, Jack, I'll get back to you just as soon as I've heard what Al and Susan think."

4. *Condition group members to be serious and constructive about their input by assigning responsibility for action to the originator of the idea.* Example: "Matt, since you brought up this problem and seem to have a lot of interest in it, please explore it thoroughly and report back to us next week with your proposed solution." This strategy allows serious concerns to surface while reducing frivolous griping.

5. *Lend support to neglected views.* Example: "Francis, you are experienced in this area and we've heard your thoughts, but it would be wise to hear the concerns of someone who is as unfamiliar with it as our customers will be. Tom, you're a novice at this; what do you see as a newcomer?"

6. *Force equal participation by using a process that requires it.* Example: "I want each of you to write down five possible solutions to this problem in the next ten minutes. Then we are going to go around the table and each person must give us one idea that has not been brought up yet. I will write them on the chart pad as we go. Remember, only one idea each time I call on you, and don't defend it, just give it. We'll discuss the merits of the ideas later. For now, let's just get as many different possibilities as we can." This approach will cause everyone to participate and allow some ideas to surface that otherwise would have remained unexpressed. Later, try ranking them by asking each member to rank their top three from all the alternatives generated.

The group process is important. The manager should identify the purpose of the meeting, explain the time frame, decide how the discussion will be organized, gather the needed information, evaluate it, and make the final decision. Any time a group member attends a meeting and does not speak, she must wonder why she was invited. Don't invite people unless you intend to consider their thoughts.

The Balancing Act

Power and participation are the two keys to effectively managing or leading a group. The manager should balance power, balance participation, and provide the process needed to achieve a team effort. The normal course of a meeting allows plenty of time to utilize the strategies suggested. Power is a natural part of management. To be effective, you need it. To protect your group, you need it. Building power is essential to goal attainment. But the involvement of all members of the team is imperative. Noninvolvement brings the feeling of powerlessness. The manager is charged with facilitating the efforts of the group. Establishing the most effective processes and norms of behavior will help the group learn how to facilitate itself.

Notes

1. Peter Drucker, as quoted on the cover of Warren Bennis and Burt Nanus, *Leaders* (New York: Harper & Row, 1985).
2. B. W. Tuckman, "Developmental Sequences in Small Groups," *Psychological Bulletin*, Vol. 63 (1965), pp. 383–399.

Action Exercise

What power bases have you been building in the organization and within your group? Which ones need more attention?

	Degree of Influence			
Power Bases	*Excellent*	*Good*	*Fair*	*Poor*
Position	_____	_____	_____	_____
Proficiency	_____	_____	_____	_____
Praise	_____	_____	_____	_____
Punishment	_____	_____	_____	_____
Preferences	_____	_____	_____	_____
Personality	_____	_____	_____	_____
Persuasion	_____	_____	_____	_____
Political skill/access	_____	_____	_____	_____

What specific actions could you take to increase your power in your weakest areas? _____

_____

Action Exercise

Analyze the participation patterns of your group.

- Who talks the most? _____
- Who talks the least? _____
- To whom does the group listen? _____
- Who is talking more than before? _____ Why? _____
- Who is talking less? _____ Why? _____
- Who is ignored by the group? _____ What can you do? _____
- Who competes? _____ Do you want them to? _____
  What can you do about it? _____
- Who cooperates? _____ Is that desirable? _____
  What can you do? _____
- What mistakes did you make in managing the last group meeting?

  _____

- How can you prevent these from happening next time?_____

  _____

Four

Managing Commitment to Get Results

Performance is in the "aye" of the beholder.

ur journey from what is to what could be is almost complete. There is one final stop to make. In Part One, I presented the kinds of "diseases" or "games" that many organizations, managers, and employees are hung up on to the detriment of performance. In Part Two, I reviewed the basics of motivation and how to build a fair, consistent, clear path to need satisfaction. In Part Three, I suggested ways of coping with yourself, with baffling bosses, and with difficult employees and discussed the effective management of groups. Now it is time for the final piece to the puzzle of performance. Having established what not to do, how to increase effort, and how to bring "difficult" people into the fold, we are ready to take the final step toward great performance—building commitment!

As we move to this level of performance, the analogy of the owner and horse becomes less and less appropriate. The human ability to use language and higher-level mental processes means that people can accomplish things that no horse, however well "managed," can achieve. Horses can't conceptualize the work and therefore must be trained and managed. But since people can conceptualize, much of the management task can readily be performed by the employees themselves. If managers persist in treating employees like horses, they will deprive themselves, the employees, and the corporation of the benefits that could accrue from communication and commitment.

Part Three was about turning on turned-off employees. Part Four suggests how to turn on performance by learning how to turn employees loose. Turning horses loose doesn't get the task done. Turning people loose can accomplish unheard-of levels of performance. When employees are involved and committed and feel that they own a piece of the action, they move toward the goals on their own. This section is about freeing up employees and managers alike.

To do this successfully, a manager must first overcome two basic fears:

1. The fear that subordinates will loaf if turned loose
2. The fear that the manager will lose control

The first fear that must be addressed is the notion that employees will slough off or loaf if the manager isn't standing over them with a whip. With attitudes like this, autocratic management will become the management dinosaur of the twenty-first century. Autocratic management kills ambition and spirit. Like anything else, its usefulness is relative to the situation. But we aren't getting troops and elephants across the Alps these days. Managers must learn to operate in a knowledge-based, service economy where change is dynamic and innovation imperative. When you tell me what to do, I don't have ownership in the outcome, you do! When I have a boring job to do, I wait around for you to give me further orders; why rush into more boredom? But when I am given the opportunity to learn, to develop, to achieve and I perceive myself as an owner, I will often perform beyond your dreams.

If you turn turned-on workers loose, they will usually achieve more than what you would have asked of them. When the manager sets up the targets, employees only work up to those levels. When an involved, committed employee sets the goals, the sky is the limit.

The second fear that must be addressed is the fear that the manager will lose control of the employees and of the work situation. If turned loose, what will they need the manager for? Exactly! My point is that when the manager gives responsibility and authority to his subordinates, instead of "riding herd" on them and redoing their work, they can manage themselves. And the manager, freed from his checking-up functions, can plan, organize, lead, and coordinate, which is what he should have been doing all along.

The Magic of Ownership

The next time you question the magic of ownership, ask yourself how many times you have seen someone polish a rented car.

Ownership is magic! The free enterprise system is built on this idea. When you own something, you are much more likely to protect it and perfect it. You can see the pride in the eyes of an owner. Lately, there have been numerous examples of what happens when management tries to retain all the power and ownership in its own hands—defective products and sloppy service, among other ills. When employees are told that it's not their car and to shut up and follow orders, sooner or later these employees will get the message and quit trying to polish management's car. When workers do specialized little tasks in the construction of an automobile and are paid by the hour, it's not their car.

Two productive ways of sharing power and ownership in an organization are through participation and delegation.

The Art of Using Participation

The value of employee participation has been debated for decades. Because of some success stories involving the use of participation, it is today increasingly scrutinized as a tool for enhancing performance. Although allowing workers to take part in decisions that affect their lives and jobs is sound, the effective use of participation is more complex than it might appear at first glance. The idea is not to force participation. Similarly, never to allow participation is mindless. Some relevant concepts must be understood before participation can be used effectively.

171

What Is Participation?

Participation is taking part, sharing, giving input. The employee must do or say something for participation to occur. Merely giving employees a hurried opportunity to blurt out something while you as manager continually glance at your watch is not participation. Participation can range from an informal conversation at the watercooler to formalized organizational programs such as consensus decision making, shared goal setting, autonomous work groups, and quality circles. At the core of this sharing is a meeting of minds, a respect for the ideas and opinions of other people. The form can range from subordinate-centered to supervisor-centered. The true essence of participation is a "climate" where an honest give-and-take is reinforced.

Manipulation is not participation. Some organizations pretend to encourage participation while actually placating. The process is not honest; rather, it is an attempt to appease and manipulate. In the "placating game," the following occurs:

- Management pretends to ask for input when the issues have already been decided.
- Input is requested only on insignificant matters.
- Participation is forced on people.
- Little time is allotted to the process, showing the low priority it has in management's eyes.

In this unfairly controlled setting, real progress is doomed. Who is kidding whom? Employees are quite capable of seeing through this fog. I once had the displeasure of being involved in a meeting called by the president to announce what was to be the single most important issue facing the company that year—participative planning! The only problem was that the president didn't show up for the meeting. Obviously he had something more important to do. Now what message do you suppose his absence sent through that auditorium? Ho hum, business as usual.

The Price and Profit of Participation

There are costs and benefits attached to any choice. Using participation has a price tag; so does not using it. Let's see if the profits outweigh the price.

The major cost attached to a participative environment is time. Gathering input from employees takes more time than not asking their advice. On the up side, time spent involving employees in decisions that directly affect them saves time during the implementation process. Participation takes time on the front end but reduces resistance to change and therefore hastens implementation on the back side.

The second price of participation is probably the psychological threats that many managers experience, including the fear of losing control and power, anxiety about their participatory skills, a reluctance to deal with well-informed subordinates, and the inability of a "get it done" mentality to embrace input and planning. Concomitantly, subordinates may reject invitations to participate owing to their conditioning or preference for being told what to do, the fear of accepting responsibility, skepticism regarding the process, a fear of the unknown, feelings of inadequacy, or a lack of incentives to become involved. On the other hand, many managers and subordinates embrace participation as a welcome opportunity for improving the work setting and work outputs.

A payoff from participation is the growth of self-respect and confidence among subordinates. Participation can also build positive feelings about management. Participation can bring more clarity to what both management and employees are doing. As communication takes place, roles, goals, and expectations of both parties come into sharper focus. Roles, goals, and expectations should be crystal clear to everyone. Unfortunately, management often shrouds them in mystery. Management by mind reading lives. The attitude that workers don't need to know the big picture, they just need to do what they are told, deprives subordinates of any chance for creativity and innovation. The rented car syndrome is reinforced.

Interactions between managers and employees afford a marvelous opportunity for challenging employees. Participation can have a positive effect on achievement. The employee who is challenged may exceed rather than just meet the formal goals. This new level of performance depends on the sincerity of the involvement and the reinforcement of outstanding behavior when it occurs. Make no mistake about it, incentives must be provided. This is new stuff to employees and if rewards don't accompany the change, they will know that "management speaks with forked tongue."

Another payoff of participation is the real possibility that commitment may develop. Having a voice in issues that affect us usually brings a stronger feeling of obligation to whatever decision is made.

Participation takes time and is not welcomed by everyone. But most people welcome it. Participation clarifies the roles, goals, and expectations in the workplace and enhances employee involvement in and commitment to the job and the company. When administered properly, participation means profits.

When Should Participation Be Used?

Participation is not a cure-all. Like most things in life, its effectiveness depends on the circumstances.

Does anyone besides you want to participate? That's the first thing you should get input on from your employees. Also, where do they feel their participation would be most desirable. An autocratic decision that everyone must now participate defeats the very premise of sharing solutions. Ordering people to volunteer ideas is sheer folly! If there is some interest in participation, allow it to occur, reinforce it, and, with luck, others will come on board when they see the benefits it produces. Not everyone wants to have input. Some people wanted it years ago but couldn't care less now. Some want to get through the few years till retirement with as little change as possible. Many are craving input. Some employees only want to have input on certain aspects of their job. Finally, our work force is so diverse that it would be unusual to find anything that was a top priority with everyone. Because most Americans were taught to be competitive rather than cooperative, the drive to differentiate oneself may be stronger than the urge to be part of the team.

As manager, consider the strength of your own desire to see participation flourish. The use of participation implies that you will seriously consider what is communicated. This doesn't mean that you will always do what your employees want. But the inference is that you will objectively and seriously evaluate all input. Unless you are willing to make this commitment to the process, don't bother fooling with participation. Closely tied to your decision will likely be the degree of confidence you have in your subordinates' abilities and ideas.

The complexity of an employee's job may influence the desirability of participation. More routine jobs may require less input by nature. Don't forget, however, that even routine jobs can be enhanced, upgraded, or eliminated. The more complex tasks may require more communication to achieve organizational goals. The really complex tasks certainly necessitate communication between the expert (employee) and the guide (manager). As a final thought, since each task is composed of several subtasks, each employee has different skill levels in these different subtasks. An employee may have great experience in one aspect of his work and be a novice in another. For example, a business school is composed of experts who should be mature in their tasks. But would you ask all of them which computer system to buy, or would you contact the computer experts and then run the decision by the general faculty to see if there were any objections?

How much time do you have before the decision is needed? There may or may not be sufficient time to solicit opinions depending on the decision deadline. If there is time, don't procrastinate until time becomes critical and then announce that there's no time for input. Deceit breeds deceit.

The type and length of discussions with subordinates are usually determined by the manager's perceptions of individual abilities, skills, and roles. In the downtime between decisions, mentor your subordinates. Build their skills and your confidence in their abilities.

Finally, employees will be watching to see what actually happens. Positive behavior must be followed by reinforcements to increase the behavior desired. There are potential intrinsic rewards in being asked, but the employee's willingness to take on more involvement must somehow be tied to the reward system. By now you presumably have a good handle on what each employee is pursuing and what consequences would be most effective in strengthening the norm of participating.

The Art of Delegating

The step beyond participation on the road to ownership is delegation. Delegation is fun stuff to ponder. To insecure managers, *delegation* is a dirty word. When insecure managers delegate, they are dismayed whatever the outcome. If the task gets done poorly, they agonize over not having done it themselves. If the task gets done really well, they feel terribly threatened. "Why do they need me?" Most managers claim to delegate but most of them don't. They think they do. The employees see it differently.

Delegation has been trumpeted as a timesaving device, as a developmental tool. It also builds trust and partnership, frees the manager to plan, and develops managerial influence. Like most of the wonder drugs, delegation requires understanding and expertise. Few managers were ever taught what and how. Delegation is misdefined and misused because it is confused with other task assignment approaches.

The key to distinguishing delegation from its many look-alikes lies in the answers to two questions:

1. How significant is the activity in question?
2. How completely did the manager "let go" of the responsibility and authority to decide?

The importance of the decision and the degree to which the manager let go of the responsibility determine what has actually transpired.

Dumping Is Not Delegating!

One of the oldest and commonest tricks in the manager's mailbox of mischief is "dumping." Dumping occurs when the manager gives a subordinate a task to do and gives her the authority to make the decision. The catch is that the task is insignificant. Making sure there is always hot coffee brewing might be an example of dumping. Many managers who think that they delegate, and announce the "fact" to others, really just dump. This manager retains all the important tasks. The jobs that get "delegated" are the uninteresting, petty ones. The manager who calls this delegating must think that his subordinates are stupid. The dumpee knows the difference. The manager usually knows the difference. Often the subordinate gets dumped on twice: First, she gets to perform an unimportant task (whoopee!); second, the manager "rewards" her by giving her another.

What is "significant" is, of course, relative. Some tasks may be boring to the manager but worthwhile for the developing subordinate. Also, menial tasks do have to be performed, and not everyone can have the luxury of doing only what is of interest. The important thing is to determine whether the subordinate views the task as a worthless activity, and not to pretend that it is delegation when it is not. Managers who constantly dump and pretend to delegate don't understand the harm they are doing. Bosses dump on subordinates, subordinates dump on their subordinates, dumpees beget dumpees.

Double Dumping Is Not Delegating!

There is, as you may have surmised, something even worse than dumping. It's called "double dumping." This managerial strategy is one that employees quickly learn to despise. The manager assigns an insignificant task (Dump 1) and makes the employee keep reporting back for approval (Dump 2). Double dumping is terribly demeaning. Waiting for your father figure to give his blessing to a task that doesn't matter to anyone—

- wastes everyone's time;
- is an expensive way to operate;
- creates animosity;
- destroys respect and trust; and
- stymies employee growth.

Double dumping is destructive, demeaning, dastardly—and besides that, it stinks! Some meaningless chores have to be done. Spread them around, but don't you dare call it delegating.

Developing Is Not Delegating!

The final nondelegation category is when a manager assigns an important task to a subordinate and requires that the subordinate bring the information gathered back to the manager who will then make the decision. The hard work is delegated. The power is retained by the manager. This technique can be used to teach and develop employees. Giving subordinates new, unfamiliar assignments is a useful way of increasing their knowledge and skills. The key to how this technique will be perceived by employees is how long it continues. Some managers use this tool effectively to help their people grow. Some managers use it all the time to keep control. Is the manager gradually increasing the employee's involvement and ability to decide on her own? Is the employee at some point allowed to decide for herself? Developing can take some of the fear out of releasing large chunks of the manager's responsibilities to his subordinates. Call it what it is! If it's development, say that. But don't pretend that this potentially useful process is delegation.

Delegation Is What It Is!

Delegation is entrusting another person with the power to act and decide the outcome of a task that is perceived by both parties as important. The reasons behind delegation are—

- to leverage the manager's influence;
- to free the manager's time for expansion;
- to teach subordinates how to handle responsibility; and
- to help subordinates learn and grow.

Proper delegation passes on authority within well-defined limits set in advance. Delegation works best in support of clear goals and accountability standards. Delegation is only feasible when coupled with training and coaching from the manager. Set the parameters, coach the employee, be available for help, positively reinforce good decisions, and require that all decisions be communicated to you. Not everyone wants more responsibility. For delegation to work well, the employee must be willing, able, and growing in confidence.

Delegation can be scary to both the manager (who is sharing some power) and the employee (who is not used to making important decisions). But in the long run, after the process and results have been smoothed out, delegation frees the manager to plan and not fight fires.

Skippy Peanut Butter: A Success Story

In general, managers and companies have underutilized delegation because they have underestimated the ability of subordinates to take on responsibility. As an example of just how far delegation has been taken in the real world, consider the Skippy Peanut Butter plant in Little Rock, Arkansas. This plant, set up thirteen years ago as an experiment after much deliberation, is basically employee-managed. It has approximately 130 workers and no line managers, in the traditional sense. There are a few managerial personnel (an administrative team) to interface with and coordinate at the division level. The workers operate in four teams of from eighteen to twenty-nine people. They are given goals and some guidelines by their parent, Best Foods. The workers decide interactively with management how to run the plant and how to meet those goals. They develop their own schedules, hire their own people by committee (regulated by management and by legal issues), and discipline their own people—with guidance from human resources. After thirteen years, they would seem to be past the experimental stage. Consistently, they have shown the highest profits, lowest costs, and highest quality of any of Best Foods' operations. Is it a miracle or an aberration? The fact that in spite of its great success this experiment has attracted relatively little attention may be silent testimony to the skepticism and/or fear that it arouses. After all, if workers can achieve goals themselves (Dr. W. Edwards Deming would agree), then why do companies have all those managers standing around?

Participation and Delegation: The Magic of Ownership!

Participation and delegation aren't necessarily for every employee. The problem is that too many managers are making the decision for their employees. If the manager doesn't believe in delegation, the employees don't get the chance to decide.

Participation and delegation are dynamic ways of empowering the work force. Participation is the first step. When employees get involved and share their ideas, they begin to feel more important to the team. Delegation allows ownership when—

- it is my task;
- it is important to the company's efforts;
- I make the decision; or
- I own it!

Whose car is it? Yours? Then I'm just a caretaker, like some CEOs of large publicly held corporations. I'm out for myself. If it's my car, then I want it to increase in value. I, like the CEO of a family-held business, am the owner. I behave differently. Wouldn't you?

Action Exercise

Think about the last week. How many times did you—

_____ encourage input from your people?

_____ make sure everyone's opinion was heard?

_____ dump assignments?

_____ double dump assignments?

_____ develop people? (and toward what end?)

_____ truly delegate?

The next step is to identify what went wrong between your good intentions and your actual behavior. Another way to put this is, in that you know what should be done, how are you stopping yourself from accomplishing it? (Be creative in your rationalizations!)

1. I stopped myself by: _____

2. I stopped myself by: _____

3. I stopped myself by: _____

Are you comfortable with these rationalizations? _____

Are your people comfortable with them? _____

Who controls your behavior?
        _____ You?   _____ Someone else?

Committed Connectedness

The kamikaze pilot embarking on his forty-ninth mission is involved but not committed.

As the statement above suggests, involvement and commitment are close, kind of like "lightning" and "lightning bug." Close and yet so far away. Commitment means a pledge to take action, to achieve results. Commitment means you don't make excuses when barriers appear; you overcome them. This chapter examines the following:

- The link between scintillating vision and commitment
- The differences between involvement, loyalty, and commitment
- Strategies for attaining higher commitment

Employees will be willing to pledge their commitment only when they see something exciting enough to warrant their enthusiasm. After employees have become participants and garnered some ownership in the organizational process, the question becomes: "How valuable is what I own? Do I own a piece of the rock or a piece of common sand?" The critical step in creating commitment is devising an organizational vision that is worthy of your employees' commitment. Management's vision of what the organization seeks to be, do, and become is commonly called the "mission." Without this attractive target, employees will only yawn instead of cheer.

Directionally Impaired Organizations

Strategic vision in organizations is a good news-bad news story. The good news is that more organizations than ever know that it is essential to create dynamic mission statements, goals, and strategies. Without these navigational and inspirational aids, organizations remain adrift. The bad news is that most of what is transpiring is merely words and attempted quick fixes.

Most organizations are underachieving because they either (1) are directionally impaired or (2) have a direction, but keep it a secret from the troops because management believes that the troops don't need to know, they just need to do! In spite of the popularity of books extolling the virtues of a grand vision and scintillating strategy as essentials to success, most organizations don't have one. Without a direction no one in the system can determine an appropriate weekly "to do" list, much less support unified annual efforts. My experience has been that if a vision exists, not many middle managers are privy to it. For too many organizations, the destination remains a mystery. Selecting coordinated targets is hard enough work when the grand scheme is clear. It is even more time-consuming and threatening when the employees are supposed to guess (management by mind reading) where they are headed.

A few organizations embrace the direction-setting process as core management stuff. For these "centered" organizations, goal setting can be an exhilarating experience because of the excitement, clarity of action, and reinforcing reward system. Noble goals are established and action plans determined. Sadly, these are the exceptions.

Most organizations aren't really goal-directed. Whatever the annual event is labeled by management, it is nothing more than an acted-out ritual. Setting difficult targets involves risk, and the possible obstacles are endless. Therefore, setting hard goals in a politically driven organization can become a do-it-yourself hangman's kit! Playing at planning has turned into one of the great American pastimes.

The Impediments to Strategic Planning

There are many reasons companies have for not creating a vision or setting goals:

- *Fear of Failure.* If they have no clear, challenging targets, they can't fail.
- *Fear of Success.* If they accept the challenge of lofty targets and achieve them, what will they have to do for an encore? The way to avoid more work, more stress, and more potential conflict is to set easy targets.
- *Fear of Mistakes.* If they set no goals, at least they won't make the mistake of picking the wrong ones.
- *Fear of Taking Risks.* If they aim for the top, they will have to take some chances. Many people are risk-aversive.
- *Fear of Objectivity.* Not setting goals means that management can evaluate the employees on whatever subjective criteria it chooses.
- *Fear of Implementation.* If they don't set goals, they can avoid the problem of how to implement them once they are determined.
- *Fear of the Unknown.* Some practicing managers prefer the comfort of the status quo, even if it means muddling through, to the unknown of a new articulated target.

The Pros of Strategic Planning

When planning is properly coordinated, each level of the organization is involved in the planning and is charged with supporting the overall vision/mission/strategy. Tough, attainable targets force employees to invest themselves energetically, assuming that the reward system supports the new direction. Strategy and goals can unite people, enhance team effort, and reward contribution. Ironically, when the vision and targets are too easy, performance is wasted and commitment becomes a joke.

The Strategic Commitment Process

The strategic commitment process is composed of seven steps. Think of it as sailing the Seven Cs!

1. *Creating the Vision.* There must be an ambitious organizational vision that will inspire and "hook" the employees. It is the responsibility of top management to create an exciting target for

the organization that necessitates greater effort on the part of all employees. There must be a *dream* that people can buy into. Being average or competitive is not very exciting stuff. Pride in one's company does not come from surviving. People want to work for something worthwhile, something grand, something exceptional. Being the best in the world at something, and doing it in a unique way, makes getting up in the morning a lot easier.

2. *Clarification.* The targets the organization is trying to achieve should be few, simple, and so clear that everyone in the organization understands them, knows them by heart, and is committed to executing them.

3. *Connectedness.* Each employee and each task must be intertwined in the accomplishment of the dream. The functioning of a football team is an excellent analogy. Each player has a defined role that is necessary to the team accomplishment. On any given play, the tasks are interrelated. The talented running back is of little value if the line doesn't block and he gets hit in the backfield. Similarly, the star salesperson is of limited value if the company can't produce, deliver on time, and service the product.

4. *Communication.* The vision and task connectedness must be enthusiastically transmitted to all employees. Every manager should be involved in the discussion of direction and the energizing of employees. This can be done by explaining the importance of the task and by instilling a sense of ownership and the impact of every job on the accomplishment of the organization's goals.

5. *Compensation.* There must be a combination of individual and team incentives. The running back can negotiate his own salary, share in the monetary rewards of the playoffs, and equally share in the glory of the championship ring. Organizations should provide individual salaries commensurate with the value of the positions and of the people filling them and further support equal sharing of all spoils (profits) from the winning effort. All members of the championship team bask in the glow of victory. Everyone is important to the victory.

6. *Control.* Measurements must be established that allow managers to track the team and individual performances in the pursuit of the target. Feedback should be specific and ongoing. How are we doing? How are you doing? How can we change things?

7. *Commitment*. A sense of commitment to a common fate must be established. Are we going to be champions or dregs? Will we establish territorial bragging rights or hang our heads at cocktail parties? Commitment, a pledge to carry out the vision, is the key to the holy grail.

What Is Commitment?

Perhaps it is best to start with what commitment is not. Commitment is not compliance, loyalty, or involvement. Compliance occurs when a manager orders a subordinate to do something and the subordinate carries out the order. The ownership is the manager's, not the employee's. The employee is merely complying with the order. This should not be mistaken for involvement or commitment.

Commitment is not loyalty. Loyalty is the sense of belonging, a willingness to remain with the organization, and the tendency to speak positively about the organization in public. Loyalty is valuable, but does not necessarily encourage initiative or creative thinking. In fact, loyalty to organizations as we once knew it may be dying out. The new breed of workers is better educated and has higher expectations. These employees are human beings first and workers second. This trend coupled with the massive acquisitions, buyouts, and mergers of recent years and the accompanying reorganizations and downsizings (layoffs) have driven a spike in the heart of loyalty. How can you be loyal to a company that has done nothing concrete to prevent the displacement of significant portions of its work force?

Commitment is not involvement. Involvement means participation and interest. Involvement does not directly translate into task dedication. Involved workers feel some sense of responsibility to produce adequate levels of quality and quantity, but they may not decide to take the final step. Involved employees can easily switch jobs or companies as the opportunity arises.

Commitment is the act of being physically, psychologically, and emotionally impelled. Commitment takes precedence over all other activities. Commitment means the worker gladly gives up other options. Commitment means making the task the top priority in one's life. Think about the difference between going steady and marriage. Going steady is involvement. Getting married is commitment. Commitment can scare people. Empowering employees, task ownership, and buying in to an exciting mission encourage commitment.

Strategies for Gaining Commitment

There are several actions a manager can take to help make commitment happen. Before doing anything else, he must first of all share several things with employees:

• *Respect.* The organizational philosophy usually needs to be overhauled. Employees at all levels must perceive that management respects them, their ideas, and their dedication. An open, honest, participative culture is required to encourage employees to share ideas to which management will then give careful consideration. Long-term organizational competitiveness and health depend on employee innovation. The people on the firing lines know what is right and wrong with the products and services they produce. But before they will contribute, they have to perceive that their ideas will receive serious attention and that there is something in it for them.

• *Responsibility.* For employees to take a more active role in decision making, companies must share much more information than they have up to now. Sales, profits, costs, purchases, and strategic goals for the coming year should be shared. Everyone must understand the big picture before they can make meaningful suggestions. If management still wants to keep company activities secret, it can forget about effecting any significant degree of involvement.

• *Information.* Teams should be formed to incorporate the various functional areas. The idea is to share information and to break down the walls created by years of departmental balkanization. As education and exposure increase, mutual respect and trust may arise.

• *Rewards.* To change behavior, the new behavior must be reinforced. Adjust the reward system to encourage involvement, loyalty, and especially commitment. If management isn't willing to change the reward system, then it's not being serious about commitment.

• *Loyalty.* No one should ever lose a job because of a helpful suggestion. If you want loyalty, you must be loyal. Educate your people, train your people, cross-train your people. Help your employees to grow into better and more demanding jobs. If I could eliminate a boring job and exchange it for a more challenging position, I'd do it in a minute. Wouldn't you? All employees should be trying to eliminate their current jobs in order to move to better ones. Cost reduction, quality improvement, and productivity depend on this attitude.

A team is an interconnected group of employees who share and shape goals, and the manager is the critical link between teams. The manager is the "thinking pin" between the plan and the output. This interface is critical for—

- gathering resources for your people;
- giving support where needed;
- clarifying roles, goals, and expectations;
- treating team members equally; and
- keeping the communication channels open.

Once employees buy in to a goal, the target becomes the overriding factor in their work lives. Managing then becomes easy because the target in essence serves as the boss. The manager in these new conditions is merely a facilitator who helps people achieve.

It is only fitting that what goes around comes around. Those organizations that reward effort get effort. Those organizations that exhibit loyalty inspire loyalty. Those organizations that involve people garner ideas. Those organizations that encourage ownership build pride. And those organizations that take the time to articulate a clear, exciting vision of the future get people to commit their talents and energy to making it happen.

Action Exercise

How much of your time do you spend inspiring—

____ Compliance?

____ Involvement?

____ Loyalty?

____ Commitment?

Write down three things that you could do tomorrow morning to encourage commitment from your people.

1. I could: _____

2. I could: _____

3. I could: _____

What resources do your people need and how can you get more of them? _____

_____

____ Are you a team? ____ How would you know?

____ Have you made the goal the boss?

If you started a Commitment Club, which of your people should belong? _____

_____

_____

16

Blood, Sweat, and Cheers

Have you ever heard of a manager who when dying said, "I wish I had spent more time working"?

ow what? After all the thinking I've asked you to do and all the performance goals your subordinates have achieved, what's next? Celebration!

Organizations currently operate in an era of doing more, with fewer resources, for less cost, with greater efficiency, and in less time. In this stressful climate, most organizations still do very little to reward people for taking care of business. The push for running "lean and mean" is accompanied by even less time for celebrating. Many companies have taken the fun out of being an employee. As Chapter 11 pointed out, we act as if praising would break our faces. As Chapter 14, on ownership, implied, creativity and fun go hand in hand. The "what have you done for me lately?" mentality can become both gruesome and boring. As employees quickly realize, if you run faster, management just cranks up the speed of the treadmill. Treating people in a way you wouldn't want your horse treated is ultimately its own reward. You will get what you give. After all the blood, sweat, and tears, where are the cheers?

Stopping to celebrate a hard-fought victory has many advantages:

- Celebration fulfills human needs for achievement, recognition, and self-esteem.
- Celebration helps the team and organizational bonding process.

190

- Celebration allows for the downtime needed to reenergize our batteries.
- Celebration shows appreciation and builds respect among participating members.
- Celebration gives value to the effort.

It's very easy for an employee in an unhealthy organization to come to the conclusion that work is overrated! Certainly, constant stress and pain are overrated! Besides ulcers and a nasty disposition, it creates a no-win situation for employees. When they don't have ownership, the game is obvious and they laugh and slow down. When they feel some ownership but are continually pressed for more effort, employees know that they are being used. Who is kidding whom?

Barriers to Celebration

The unwillingness to stop and enjoy the fruits of our labors is reinforced by three *P* words: *pressure, perfection,* and *pettiness.*

1. *Pressure.* In a competitive environment, the tendency is to achieve the goal and immediately move on to the next task. Time moves on, so must we. This compulsive behavior flies in the face of what we know to be true. People learn most effectively for short periods of time. Concentration wanes and energy is depleted as the length of focus increases. Because workers now look at work as only a part of their lives, breaks and celebration become even more significant. Employees are well aware of "burnout" and will experience it in their professions. No downtime brings quicker burnout!

2. *Perfection.* The pursuit of perfection is another convenient reason for not celebrating. Since no performance is perfect, there is always something to correct, something to change to make the next effort better. Is a 98 out of 100 a great score that warrants some joy, or a failure driving you back to the drawing board to fix the mistake on the two points? Striving for excellence is a noble goal. Being unable to appreciate super advances toward that goal creates a depressing climate in which human needs remain unsatisfied. People can tell when they're being used. Lack

of recognition will eventually cost an organization some of its best performers.

3. *Pettiness.* The win-lose ethic in many organizations creates a narrow, nasty environment in which trifling jealousies flourish. Individual competition makes it difficult for employees to acknowledge the accomplishments of others. Each personal victory represents a defeat for someone else. If you think I'm exaggerating, ask yourself how you would react to a great achievement by one of your peers. Would you be able to accept it as an accomplishment worth praising? Could you sincerely feel happy for that person? Or would you feel that you were losing the battle, that your colleague had shown you up? In the win-lose environment, the concept of a "team" is next to impossible to treat seriously.

Celebration: Blood, Sweat, and Cheers

As manager, you can make a difference. At least at your own level you can create an atmosphere in which recognition and respect prevail. Commitment can be grown and valued. People deserve to be treated as more than horses. Human performance demands human understanding.

Here are three possible strategies for creating the proper performance environment. Choose the ones you can believe in and pull off.

1. *Praise, praise, praise.* Go out of your way to find valid performance issues to recognize. Make winners out of your people by creating positive self-images. Why not start your staff meetings with a "reward" session? Reinforce what is going well. Congratulate your superperformers. Learn to give and accept praise gracefully. Create meaningful, attainable goals and rewards. Wouldn't it be marvelous if we all did well? Don't underestimate the importance of your personal recognition. People feel more powerful when they have close contact with and positive reinforcement from their mentor. So pat your people on the back. Buy them coffee. Nominate them for some recognition. Thank their families. By the way, these aren't "atta boys" or "atta girls." They're thank-you notes!

2. *Become human.* It is great therapy for the troops to see their manager as a human being. Your striking out at a softball game will bring them great joy. Because you have more power, more money, more status, and more responsibility than your employees, they need to see you as one of them. Breaking the ice at work during stressful times can be valuable. You may not want to go as far as the manager who pulled out a water gun and shot one of his people and then handed the water gun to that person and encouraged him to shoot back to break the tension. Find your own way to make your subordinates feel more comfortable with the setting and more in control of the situation.

3. *Form a club.* Becoming a member of an exclusive club is attractive to people. Create your own club. Call the club whatever makes sense in your setting. Perhaps "The E [for excellence] Team," maybe membership in "The Wall of Fame." Why not "The Honorary Doctors of Dedication," or "The Commitment Club," or "Hogan's Heroes/Heroines"? Have fun naming it. Be creative! Devise your own criteria and induction procedures. Make the membership meaningful. Build the employee's sense of importance, involvement, contribution, and commitment.

EPILOGUE
Meanwhile, Back at the Ranch

While you were reading this book, what was going on back at your shop? No one else read this book, just you. In one way, that's much better than attending a seminar. When you go away for three days to attend sessions on whatever the new management fad happens to be, the troops back home are awaiting your return and dreading your new behavior. They know that you will come back full of some crazy new ideas. They merely wait for the first crisis to hit. Under pressure, managers usually revert to the old ways. The employees can then breathe a sigh of relief: "Ah, he's back to normal. I knew the vaccination wouldn't take."

Reading this book gives you a better chance to ease into a few new behaviors. Your employees' expectations haven't been altered yet.

What will you do when you get back to the shop with the same old people, the same old pressures, the same old biases? What will you try? How long will it last? Will you need to be revaccinated? The only way you will really change is if you make a commitment—a pledge stating the specific behavior you will exhibit—and check on yourself to see how you did.

Action Exercise

1. What specific behaviors do you promise to change during your next day at work?

      I will: _____

      I will: _____

      I will: _____

2. At the end of the day, reflect on your performance.

      What worked well? _____

      _____

      What didn't work well? _____

      _____

      How can you improve next time? _____

      _____

GOOD LUCK!

Permissions Acknowledgments

I gratefully acknowledge permission from the following publishers to adapt, expand, and reprint some of my previously published materials.

AMA Periodicals, New York. Reprinted, by permission of the publisher, from *Personnel:* Ken Matejka and Dick Dunsing, "Managing Baffling Bosses" (February 1989), pp. 46–50; Ken Matejka and Dick Dunsing, "Opening Doors: Good Relationships Mean Good Management" (September 1988), pp. 74–78; Ken Matejka and Dick Dunsing, "The Mystique of Macho Management" (July 1987), pp. 62–66; and Ken Matejka, Neil Ashworth, and Dianne Dodd-McCue, "Managing Difficult Employees: Challenge or Curse?" (July 1986), pp. 43–46. All rights reserved.

AMA Periodicals, New York. Reprinted, by permission of the publisher, from *Supervisory Management:* Ken Matejka, Neil Ashworth, and Dianne Dodd-McCue, "Discipline Without Guilt" (May 1986), pp. 34–36; and Ken Matejka and Audrey Guskey Federouch, "The Supervisor as Strategic Leader" (forthcoming). All rights reserved.

National Management Association, Dayton, Ohio. Reprinted, by permission of the publisher, from *Manage:* Ken Matejka and Dick Dunsing, "The Delegation Matrix" (Spring 1987), pp. 5–7; and Ken Matejka and Jay Liebowitz, "A Commitment to Ex-Sell" (February 1989), pp. 2–6. All rights reserved.

Pace Communications, Greensboro, N.C.: Reprinted, by permission of the publisher, from *PACE:* Ken Matejka and Neil Ashworth, "Corporate Diseases of Excellence" (August 1985), pp. 49–52. All rights reserved.

Administrative Management Society, Trevose, Pa. Reprinted, by permission of the publisher, from *Management World:* Ken Matejka and Kurt Rethwisch, "Creativity: Myths and Solutions" (January-February

1989). pp. 47, 52; Ken Matejka and Dick Dunsing, "To the Rescue: Crisis Managers and Crisis Don't Mix" (July-August 1988), pp. 39–40; Ken Matejka and Dick Dunsing, "Time Management: Changing Some Traditions" (March-April 1988), pp. 6–7; Ken Matejka and Neil Ashworth, "Managing Praise: Take a Bow" (April-May 1987), pp. 22–24; Ken Matejka and Dick Dunsing, "Great Expectations" (January 1987), pp. 16–17; and Ken Matejka and Dick Dunsing, "Holding Out for a Hero" (March 1986), pp. 42–44. All rights reserved.

Dalton Communications, New York. Reprinted, by permission of the publisher, from *Administrative Management:* Ken Matejka and Dick Dunsing, "Managing Employee Rewards" (June 1986), pp. 22–24; and Ken Matejka and Neil Ashworth, "The Employee's Hierarchy of Greeds" (October 1985), pp. 24–25. All rights reserved.

Clinical Laboratory Management Association, Paoli, Pa. Reprinted, by permission of the publisher, from *Clinical Management Laboratory Review:* Ken Matejka and John South, "Practical Strategies for Leading an Effective Group" (July-August 1989), pp. 221–224. All rights reserved.

MCB University Press, UK. Reprinted, by permission of the publisher, from *Journal of Managerial Psychology:* Ken Matejka, Neil Ashworth, and Dianne Dodd-McCue, "Managing the Difficult Boss" (March-April 1988), pp. 3–7. Also, excerpts from *Management Decisions:* Ken Matejka and Dick Dunsing, "Fad Labelling—The Curse That Can Kill Organizational Change," Vol. 27 (1989), pp. 37–39. All rights reserved.

National Research Bureau, Burlington, Ia. Reprinted, by permission of the publisher, from *Supervision:* Ken Matejka, Neil Ashworth, and Dianne Dodd-McCue, "Pay for Performance Versus Performance for Pay" (April 1989), pp. 14–16; and Ken Matejka and Jay Liebowitz, "Five Critical Challenges to Communicating Clearly" (February 1989), pp. 9–10. All rights reserved.

Prentice-Hall, Inc., Englewood Cliffs, N.J. Reprinted, by permission of the publisher, from Ken Matejka, *Handling Human Performance,* 1981. All rights reserved.

Index

[Italics (e.g., *53*) refer to graphic material.]